TO EIRLYS

JOHN MARSTON'S PLAYS

Theme, Structure and Performance

JOHN MARSTON'S PLAYS

Theme, Structure and Performance

MICHAEL SCOTT

First published by
THE MACMILLAN PRESS LTD
London and Basingstoke
Associated companies in Delhi
Dublin Hong Kong Johannesburg Lagos
Melbourne New York Singapore Tokyo

Phototypeset in V.I.P. Palatino by
Western Printing Services Ltd, Bristol, England
and printed in Hong Kong

British Library Cataloguing in Publication Data

Scott, Michael
John Marston's plays
1. Marston, John, b.1576 – Criticism and interpretation
I. Title
822'.3 PR2697

ISBN 0–333–21909–0

Contents

Acknowledgements

I am grateful to the editor of *Trivium* for permission to reprint material from 'Dreams and Dramatic Technique: John Marston's *Antonio* Plays', *Trivium*, XI (1975); to Methuen & Co. Ltd for permission to quote from *The Elizabethan Dumb Show,* by D. Mehl; and to Chatto & Windus for permission to quote from *English Dramatic Form,* by M. C. Bradbrook. I am very thankful to Dr. G. I. Williams of the University of Wales, who has read through draft copies of the work and has given me invaluable advice throughout; to Miss T. M. O'Reilly, who has deciphered my hand so as to produce the typescript; and to my wife, who has read, reread and discussed the work more times than I can remember.

M.S.

1
Introduction: Text and Interpretation

Over the last three decades there has been a considerable revival of interest in Marston, with a number of scholars engaging in lively debates about the way in which we should approach his drama. The most recent of these discussions has been accommodated in the pages of *Essays in Criticism*,[1] where Richard Levin issued a warning that too many critics were beginning to excuse bad plays with their proposals that the works were parodies and satires of other dramas. R. A. Foakes's evaluation of Marston[2] was cited as an example, and consequently Foakes replied conceding the presence of the danger but stating that 'evidence' for a decision about a Renaissance play's nature is difficult to find one way or another since, 'For the most part, there are only the texts of plays, which critics have had no opportunity of seeing in performance.' This in turn led Levin to confirm his 'basic principle of interpretation':

> I do approach the plays of this period with the assumption that they are to be treated as 'straight' – as meaning what they seem to mean – unless there is very good evidence, internal or external, to the contrary. And I make this assumption because I believe it describes the attitude or mental 'set' which audiences actually bring to plays when encountering them for the first time (at least up to very recently), and which dramatists, including ironic dramatists, count on when writing them. If we do not begin with some such normal expectation (which is of course subject to all sorts of modification as the evidence of the play unfolds before us), then any artistic difficulty or defect in any work can be transmuted into a positive virtue by the philosopher's stone of parody, and we are thrown into . . . critical chaos.[3]

Levin's argument cannot be dismissed. We must base our evaluation of a play on the firmest foundation possible, which quite naturally has to be the text. But, although the soundest basis available, it must be remembered that a play's text is very different from that of a novel or a poem. Where Levin seems to be misled is in the implicit assumption that there is a necessary equation between good drama and literature. In some cases, especially Shakespeare, this may be so, but it does not necessarily have to be the case. Plays first and foremost have to be judged on criteria appropriate to their lives on stage rather than on the printed page. Marston writes in his preface to *The Malcontent*:

> For the rest of my supposed tartness, I fear not but unto every worthy mind it will be approved so general and honest as may modestly pass with the freedom of a satire. I would fain leave the paper; only one thing afflicts me, to think that scenes invented merely to be spoken should be enforcively published to be read, and that the least hurt I can receive is to do myself the wrong. But, since others otherwise would do me more, the least inconvenience is to be accepted. I have myself therefore set forth this Comedy; but so, that my enforced absence must much rely upon the printer's discretion; but I shall entreat slight errors in orthography may be as slightly over-passed, and that the unhandsome shape which this trifle in reading presents may be pardoned for the pleasure it once afforded you when it was presented with the soul of lively action.

Plays should be remembered by their 'lively action', and their honesty, in Marston's case, should be 'approved' by the criteria of satiric freedom. The first objection to this is, of course, that we do not often have the opportunity of seeing Marston's plays in 'action', and we might make the corollary that when we do see them the director's interpretation is often not akin to our own. Consequently we tend to designate it as a 'poor production'. All this raises fundamental problems about the way in which we approach dramatic texts generally.

It is interesting to remember that Chekhov disapproved of Stanislavsky's interpretation of his plays since the director turned the dramatist's comedies into naturalistic tragedies. Meyerhold forcibly held similar objections.[4] Yet when Livanov created a new production of *The Seagull* for the Moscow Art Theatre he was criticised for swinging too far in the other direction: it was too comic.[5] If directors and dramatists actually staging plays can have such divergent interpretations and aims for twentieth-century drama,[6] the problem of deciphering the intention behind Renaissance texts must at least be as great. When, as drama critics, we allow a play-text to 'unfold before us', we must be constantly aware that it is doing so in a manner peculiar to dramatic art. Unlike the novelist or poet, or even the sculptor or painter, the dramatist is never in total control of his medium of expression.[7] The text is only one component of the play; the *mise en scene* is another; but the personalities, decisions and creativity of the director and actors are others, as is the presence and natural participation of the audience. All are involved and are essential to that event which we call 'the play'. Consequently the academic critic confronting a play-text in his study has in front of him just one element of a vastly complicated art form. He should not rely solely, therefore, on the traditional instruments of literary criticism to make his evaluation, but should more appropriately employ approaches used by the theatre director. As Stanislavsky notes, many of these do involve literary criticism,[8] but they go further. We must assimilate and evaluate the text and the conventions to which it belongs, but like a director and actor we must extend our knowledge to creative interpretation. If plays live in production, then within our imagination we have to stage the play, becoming both actors and audience. This does not lead to 'critical chaos', but to interpretative critical evaluation, often producing a great variety of equally sound views about a play. If directors can fundamentally disagree in their productions of drama and yet each produce a worthwhile performance, so dramatic critics should likewise be able to present totally different views about the nature of a Marston or a Shakespeare or a Chekhov play, in so far as in doing so they do not tamper with or alter that other component of the play, the text.

It seems that this is exactly what has happened in another of the major critical debates over Marston, that between G. K. Hunter[9] and, once again, R. A. Foakes. Both have employed the text and conventions of the Elizabethan theatre as a basis for imaginative critical interpretations. Hunter's research into the tragicomic form has consequently set a firm foundation for further criticism to examine the practical purpose of a duality of tone in production. Similarly, Foakes's and also Anthony Caputi's[10] realisation of the satiric nature of drama in the Elizabethan private theatres shows a relationship with the manner in which Jonathan Miller produced *The Malcontent* at Nottingham in 1973.[11] In approaching a play as ambiguous in its text as *Antonio's Revenge* both Hunter and Foakes may be correct, therefore, in their respective views as to how the work should be interpreted as a play. It may be a satire on certain theatrical conventions; it may be a serious but new approach towards tragedy or towards tragicomedy; or it could be a complicated union of all these elements. The only one who can decide is the director or the critic-as-director. The latter, like any professional in the theatre, has to find a viable 'through line' for the drama; a consistent interpretation which is in harmony as far as possible with elusive textual evidence, thus producing a whole rather than a farrago. If this can be done in a number of ways with Marston, as it certainly can with Chekhov and Shakespeare, so much the better. Consequently the present work is an attempt to see 'life' in Marston's drama rather than regarding it as mere historical documentation. It must depend therefore on a personal interpretation, but one which necessarily and gratefully acknowledges the work of previous Marston critics as well as the foundation of the texts.[12]

2
Actor, Priest and Rite

In *An Actor Prepares* Stanislavsky advocates a system of acting which in its philosophy echoes a moral concern about the actors' profession such as has worried mankind from Plato onwards. This problem can be seen to be a key to our understanding of Marston's *Antonio* plays. Stanislavsky proposes that an actor must have a personal affinity with his part; that in order to portray a role he must be able 'to recall sensations previously experienced'[1] in his own life, so as to give his part validity. Thus, to a great extent the actor of Hamlet must be Hamlet himself:

> When a real artist is speaking the soliloquy 'to be or not to be', is he merely putting before us the thoughts of the author and executing the business indicated by his director? No, he puts into the lines much of his own conception of life.
>
> Such an artist is not speaking in the person of an imaginary Hamlet. He speaks in his own right as one placed in the circumstances created by the play. The thoughts, feelings, conceptions, reasoning of the author are transformed into his own. And it is not his sole purpose to render the lines so that they shall be *understood*. For him it is necessary that the spectators *feel* his inner relationship to what he is saying. They must follow his own creative *will* and desires. Here the motive forces of his psychic life are united in action and interdependent.
>
> (*An Actor Prepares*, pp. 248–9)

It is this psychic interdependency of actor and role which is the basis of Antonio's moral conduct in both the *Antonio* plays and the metaphor through which the majority of the characters express themselves. Some of the problems of the relationship are first expressed comically in the Induction to *Antonio and Mellida* where the actors discuss their parts. Antonio, for example, complains that he is to appear as an Amazon:

Antonio	I was never worse fitted since the nativity of my actorship; I shall be hiss'd at, on my life now.
Feliche	Why, what must you play?
Antonio	Faith, I know not what, an hermaphrodite, two parts

in one; my true person being Antonio son to the Duke of Genoa, though for the love of Mellida, Piero's daughter, I take this feigned presence of an Amazon, calling myself Florizel and I know not what. I a voice to play a lady! I shall ne'er do it.

Alberto . . . Not play two parts in one? away, away; 'tis common fashion. Nay, if you cannot bear two subtle fronts under one hood, idiot go by, go by, off this world's stage. O time's impurity!

Antonio Ay, but when use hath taught me action to hit the right point of a lady's part, I shall grow ignorant, when I must turn young prince again, how but to truss my hose.

(*A & M*, Induction, 65–72, 73–9)[2]

Humorously Antonio hits on the problem: once you have become your part and have established the psychic interdependency, how do you return to the normality of your former role? By the conclusion of *Antonio's Revenge* Antonio and his fellow revengers have become so dependent on their roles of vengeance that they cannot return to their former selves. The comedy has transformed into a tragedy which is only relieved by what at first sight seems to be the obscure metaphor of the monastery. To illustrate how this happens I shall trace the development of three characters (or character types) in the plays: Pandulpho, Piero and Antonio.

As G. K. Hunter has noted, Pandulpho, who appears only in *Antonio's Revenge*, may be seen thematically as a continuation and extension of the parts played by Andrugio and Feliche in *Antonio and Mellida*.[3] All three are Stoics who endure the horror of life through a close adherence to rational philosophy. But it is made clear that in doing so they are acting parts, not in terms of affected passion but in terms of affected reason. Thus Pandulpho is able to answer Alberto's rebuke that he is not mourning for his son by stating that he is not an emotional actor:

Would'st have me cry, run raving up and down
For my son's loss? Would'st have me turn rank mad,
Or wring my face with mimic action,
Stamp, curse, weep, rage, and then my bosom strike?
Away, 'tis apish action, player-like.

(*AR*, I. ii. 312–16)

He is no actor in the Hieronimo tradition, but the cool philosopher. Hunter points out that, with Feliche, Pandulpho is 'the only possible alternative to the world of flattery, corruption, and power', and continues by saying that in Venice their Stoicism 'was so pure that it was difficult to see what they were doing at the court of the tyrant Piero.'[4] Marston, however, makes plain the reason for their presence. Their philosophy is so pure that it cannot be valid. It is an act which they falsely employ to disguise their basic feelings and emotions; their real selves. This is illustrated by the way in which the Stoic posture is satirised.[5] Feliche, for example, is seen to take a high moral stand concerning the decadence of the court, but exposes his apostasy when he grows envious of the fop Castilio's success with women:

> Confusion seize me, but I think thou liest.
> Why should I not be sought to then as well?
> Fut! methinks I am as like a man.
> Troth! I have a good head of hair, a cheek
> Not as yet wan'd, a leg, faith, in the full.
>
> (*A & M*, III. ii. 68–72)

Similarly, Andrugio's resolve to find a substitute and better kingdom in a majesty of the spirit and contentment with the world of nature is, when his servant enrages him by merely mentioning the people whom he once ruled, exposed as being the creation of a poseur:

> Name not the Genoese; that very word
> Unkings me quite, makes me vile passion's slave . . .
> Was never prince with more applause confirm'd,
> With louder shouts of triumph launched out
> Into the surgy main of government;
> Was never prince with more despite cast out,
> Left shipwreck'd, banish'd, on more guiltless ground.
> . . . Alas, one battle lost,
> Your whorish love, your drunken healths, your hoots and shouts,
> Your smooth 'God Save's,' and all your devils, last,
> That tempts our quiet to your hell of throngs –
> Spit on me, Lucio, for I am turn'd slave;
> Observe how passion domineers o'er me.
>
> (*A & M*, IV. i. 68–9, 72–6, 79–84)

The swift juxtaposing of the Stoicism with the passion exposes and satirises the folly of the 'wise man's' former sententious stance, which indeed would have been intensified by the satiric portrait's being drawn by a child actor.

These however, are minor cases of apostasy in comparison with Pandulpho. From his first appearance in *Antonio's Revenge* he is presented as the man whose philosophy raises him above emotional distress. Thus he refuses to grieve for his son's death but instead laughs:

> 'tis not true valor's pride
> To swagger, quarrel, swear, stamp, rave, and chide,
> To stab in fume of blood, to keep loud coil,
> To bandy factions in domestic broils,
> To dare the act of sins whose filth excels
> The blackest customs of blind infidels.
> No, my lov'd youth, he may of valor vaunt
> Whom fortune's loudest thunder cannot daunt,
> Whom fretful galls of chance, stern fortune's siege
> Makes not his reason slink, the soul's fair liege,
> Whose well-peis'd action ever rests upon
> Not giddy humours, but discretion.
> (*AR*, I. ii. 323–34)

Marston seems to show an approval for such an attitude and we could postulate that this is a condemnation by the dramatist of the 'acts of sin' and 'filth' in which his characters are later to indulge. Pandulpho is to become one of these revengers; so Marston, displaying a duality of vision, presents the character as superficially Stoic but in real terms passionate. Thus, when Pandulpho is confronted with Piero, the latter becomes confused and angry at the appearance of the Stoic's virtue:

> He is a virtuous man; what has our court to do
> With virtue, in the devil's name!
>
> Hence doting stoic! By my hope of bliss,
> I'll make thee wretched.
>
> Would I were deaf! O plague! Hence, dotard wretch,
> Tread not in court! All thou hast I seize.
> (*AR*, II. i. 90–1, 134–5, 165–6)

But beneath all this appearance the weak foundation is being hinted at. Why does Pandulpho have to laugh in order to overcome his grief? By going to the other extreme from tears he is overacting and so implicitly exposing his true feeling. Thus his wise maxims on the same occasion seem forced and contrived:

> Piero How now, Pandulpho, weeping for thy son?

Pandulpho No, no, Piero, weeping for my sins;
Had I been a good father he had been
A gracious son.
(*AR*, II. i. 63–6)

Yet in the early stages of the play, the most telling indication of the falsity of Pandulpho's stance emerges in his secret encouragement of Antonio's passion. In Act II, scene i, Pandulpho joins with others in a sinister and emotionally volatile chorus of woe:

Mellida [*Within*] Ay me!
Antonio And curse –
Pandulpho [*Within*] Black powers.
Antonio And cry –
Maria [*Within*] O heaven!
Antonio And close laments with –
Alberto [*Within*] O me, most miserable!
Pandulpho [*Within*] Woe for my dear, dear son!
(*AR*, II. ii. 64–6)

It is Pandulpho's voice also that with the dead Stoics, Andrugio and Feliche, gives the revenger his command to 'Murder' (*AR*, III. i. 125–7).

Together these acts of encouragement help to give the impression that Pandulpho's philosophy is not as sound as he states. We are not surprised therefore that it is he who appears in answer to Antonio's prayer to Vengeance; he who assists Antonio's marriage with death by laying Feliche's body across the revenger's breast; and he who instructs the revenger to humiliate himself as a preparation for his coming work:

Antonio, kiss my foot; I honor thee
In laying thwart my blood upon thy breast
I tell thee, boy, he was Pandulpho's son,
And I do grace thee with supporting him.
(*AR*, IV. ii. 24–7)

Soon after this, as he prepares to aid the revengers in their final act of butchery, Pandulpho readily admits that his Stoicism has been false:

Man will break out, despite philosophy.
Why, all this while I ha' but play'd a part,
Like to some boy that acts a tragedy,
Speaks burly words and raves out passion;

> But when he thinks upon his infant weakness,
> He droops his eye. I spake more than a god,
> Yet am less than a man.
> I am the miserablest soul that breathes.
>
> (*AR*, IV. ii. 69–76)

His act has not been his passion, as he implicitly accused Antonio's of being, but rather it has been his purely theoretical and idealistic stand. Marston continues by showing Pandulpho's true nature to be as intensely brutal as either Piero's or Antonio's. His language degenerates (*AR*, V. ii. 28–56); he takes a grim sadistic delight in his part in Piero's murder (*AR*, V. iii. 63–115); and finally he vies with Antonio for the honour of the deed, insisting: 'By yon bright spangled front of heaven, 'twas I; / 'Twas I sluic'd out his lifeblood' (*AR*, V. iii. 124–5).

In Pandulpho's characterisation, Marston seems to anticipate a common eighteenth-century theme – that of the false philosopher; the man who attempts to divorce reason from emotion, pretending the latter does not exist.[6] In doing so he shows Pandulpho as truly adequate for Piero's horrific court and reminds us of Christ's teaching:

> When the unclean spirit is gone out of a man, he walketh through dry places, seeking rest, and findeth none. Then he saith, I will return into my house from whence I came out; and when he is come, he findeth *it* empty, swept, and garnished. Then goeth he, and taketh with himself seven other spirits more wicked than himself, and they enter in and dwell there: and the last *state* of that man is worse than the first.
>
> (Matthew, xii. 43–5)

So as to discharge the evil spirit of unregulated passion from himself, Pandulpho pretends to rationality thinking that man can discard all elements of passion. It is not a true role since there is no real affinity between it and Pandulpho's true self. The act therefore cannot be sustained. It fails as it has to do. The spirit returns, his reason breaks down and his new situation becomes worse than his first.

So to the second actor, Piero. When T. S. Eliot described Marston's major and minor characters as 'lifeless'[7] he was perhaps missing the point that the dramatist presents them in a highly stylised form. The characters generally tend towards types, reflecting their theoretical implications. This is partly true with the duke. In his character presentation throughout most of *Antonio and Mellida*, Marston employs a traditional form for the tyrant prince. He is to 'be proud, stroke up the hair and strut' (*A & M*, Induction, 14). Thus like a tyrant from an old mystery cycle, Piero's first appearance shows him wallowing in his pride and placing himself amongst the gods:

> Victorious Fortune, with triumphant hand,
> Hurleth my glory 'bout this ball of earth,
> Whilst the Venetian Duke is heaved up
> On wings of fair success to overlook
> The low-cast ruins of his enemies;
> To see myself ador'd and Genoa quake,
> My fate is firmer than mischance can shake.
> . . .
> *O me coelitum excelsissimum!*
> (*A & M*, I. i. 35–41, 77)

Such a stylised presentation of pride immediately establishes the duke as an irrational monarch, whose conceit is to produce much of the entertainment in the play. In particular his great joy in success is often juxtaposed with his annoyance at being tricked, thus producing the comedy. Likewise, his unregulated passion is continually exposed by his failure to keep a proper control over his tongue or even think clearly:

> Antonio his head, his head! Keep you the court; the rest stand still, or run, or go, or shout, or search, or scud, or call, or hang, or do-do-do, so-so-so-something. I know not who-who-who-what I do-do-do-nor who-who-who-where I am.
> (*A & M*, III. ii. 173–7)

This absurd lack of control over his tongue may be related to his bombastically proud language, which, in the final scene of *Antonio and Mellida*, manoeuvres him into Andrugio's plot. His emotional desire on this occasion, to destroy Andrugio and yet to appear 'munificent' to his court, leads him to make outlandish gestures:

> Conduct him with attendance sumptuous,
> Sound all the pleasing instruments of joy,
> Make triumph, stand on tiptoe whilst we meet;
> O sight most gracious, O revenge most sweet!
> . . .
> We still with most unmov'd resolve confirm
> Our large munificence, and here breathe
> A sad and solemn protestation:
> When I recall this vow, O let our house

> Be even commanded, stained and trampled on
> As worthless rubbish of nobility.
> (*A & M*, v. ii. 133–6, 140–5)

In contrast, in *Antonio's Revenge* we find a new Piero, not in character essentially, but in his ability to disguise by hypocrisy his inclination towards evil action. When alone or with only his confidant he still shows his bombast pride,[8] and, as in *Antonio and Mellida*, there is no real rational motivation given for his barbarity.[9] Yet when in the presence of the court he shows that he has learnt a feigned passion which disguises his true emotional feelings. But this is only because they find life from the truths of his world and experience. Without contradiction, therefore, he is able to say,

> There glow no sparks of reason in the world;
> All are rak'd up in ashy beastliness;
> The bulk of man's as dark as Erebus;
> No branch of reason's light hangs in his trunk;
> There lives no reason to keep league withal;
> I ha' no reason to be reasonable.
> (*AR*, I. ii, 222–7)

This is exactly right. Piero is fundamentally an emotional and irrational man; the only reason he uses is that designed to gain his irrational and unmotivated ends. It is doubtful whether such a speech could have been uttered by the Piero of *Antonio and Mellida*. Neither could that character have been able to woo Maria into such a state of mind that her husband's ghost has to appear to inform her of his (Piero's) evil (*AR*, III. ii. 62–75). Similarly, in the first play he lacks the controlled rationality of evil which in *Antonio's Revenge* can even persuade Strotzo to allow himself to be quietly strangled (*AR*, IV. i. 190).

The Piero of *Antonio's Revenge* therefore has discovered how to discipline his emotion, and this gives him, superficially, the appearance of a new man. Such a development has often led critics astray in the appreciation of the unity of the plays. Thus, for example, H. Harvey Wood wrongly asserts that, 'Although the two plays were entered and published together, it is necessary to postulate a considerable interval between their composition; an interval sufficient to allow for a complete change in the author's conception of plot and characterisation.'[10] Yet, as we see, there is no change in Piero's fundamental characterisation. The only alteration is in his new gained ability to disguise his basic self and adapt himself for his part. This act of hypocrisy, as he tells us himself, however, was not gained in *Antonio's Revenge*, but, ironically, in *Antonio and Mellida*.

There, in the concluding scene, he realised that, in order to gain his revenge over Andrugio and yet remain a seemingly magnanimous duke to his people, he had to employ the art of hypocrisy:

> Hell, Night,
> Give loud applause to my hypocrisy.
> When his bright valor even dazzled sense
> In off'ring his own head, public reproach
> Had blurr'd my name – Speak, Strotzo, had it not –
> If then I had –
>
> (*AR*, I. i. 30–5)

It was in the last, crucial scene of the play that he learned how to disguise his emotion in order to find time to gain his ends. That scene resulted in his learning the maturity of villainy which becomes so apparent in *Antonio's Revenge*. For in the *Antonio and Mellida* closing scene he capitalised on a new-found hypocritical act by feigning a false grief over the death of Antonio:

> O that my tears bedewing thy wan cheek
> Could make new spirit sprout in thy cold blood.
> . . .
> O that my life, her love, my dearest blood,
> Would but redeem one minute of his breath!
>
> (*A & M*, V. ii. 199–200, 207–8)

Piero here, paradoxically, fakes the passionate excesses which had previously led him into Andrugio's trap. Unfortunately for him, on this occasion there is a game of double double bluff, and the 'dead' Antonio, like Andrugio before him, makes use of Piero's 'passionate tongue':

> I seize that breath. Stand not amaz'd, great states;
> I rise from death that never liv'd till now.
> Piero, keep thy vow, and I enjoy
> More unexpressed height of happiness
> Than power of thought can reach. . . .
>
> (*A & M*, V. ii. 209–13)

Nevertheless, with Piero we see the man of passion who through a strange conversion learns how to disguise his emotional weakness by an evil rational guise – an act which produces much of the tragedy in the second play.

Philip J. Ayres has pointed out that 'some sort of parallel is apparently implied' by the resemblance in character of Piero and

Antonio.[11] John Peter has seen such similarity between the two as first occurring with the murder of Julio, which he complains 'simply makes one more Piero of him [Antonio]'.[12] Yet Peter immediately prior to this statement describes those characteristics of Antonio which, throughout the plays, single him out for a comparison with the duke: Antonio, he says, has a 'propensity for ranting', an 'inconsequential vagueness about his own motives for action', a 'pride in his own dejection and his own bloodthirstiness'. As we have seen, all these properties belong also to Piero. In *Antonio and Mellida* Marston in fact presents both men as having basically uncontrollable emotional characters, and consequently mocks them in similar ways. Thus, as with Piero, Antonio's histrionics are ridiculed. Four times[13] the hero of the action farcically 'falls to the ground' in an exhibition of despair – a fault to which his father, Andrugio, is also prone.[14] As with Piero, such excessive emotion is satirised through the character's inability to express himself verbally, the linguistic device of aposiopesis being employed:

What was't I said?
O, this is naught but speckling melancholy.
I have been –
That Morpheus tender skinp – Cousin german –
Bear with me good –
Mellida – Clod upon clod thus fall
Hell is beneath; yet Heaven is over all.
(*A & M*, IV. i. 23–9)[15]

Also as with Piero, Antonio's passionate extremes are abruptly juxtaposed in a manner which we associate more with a Puccini opera than with an English Renaissance play:

Antonio Father, now I have an antidote
'Gainst all the poison that the world can breathe;
My Mellida, my Mellida doth bless
This bleak waste with her presence.
[*To* page.] How now, boy,
Why dost thou weep? Alas, where's Mellida?
Page Aye me, my lord.
Antonio A sudden horror doth invade my blood;
My sinews tremble and my panting heart
Scuds round about my bosom to go out,
Dreading the assailant, horrid passion.
O, be no tyrant; kill me with one blow.
(*A & M*, IV. ii. 5–15)

The contrast on this occasion is pointed out by the continuity of the poison image, but even more interesting is that in its elaboration and emphasis on self the metaphor neatly conveys not Antonio's grief but rather his uncontrolled egoistic nature. The relationship with Piero is unmistakable.

Despite these resemblances there are to be found in *Antonio's Revenge* major differences between Antonio's development and that of Piero. Whereas in this play Piero learns how to disguise his emotional instability, Antonio, in the face of mounting horrors, rebuffs reason throughout. It is this rejection which leads to a very different kind of role-play from Piero's.

Early in the drama the fears of Antonio's companions for his health are repulsed by his inclination towards passionate excess:

> Alberto Sweet prince, be patient.
> Antonio 'Slid, sir, I will not, in despite of thee.
> Patience is slave to fools, a chain that's fix'd
> Only to posts and senseless log-like dolts.
> Alberto 'Tis reason's glory to command affects.
> Antonio Lies thy cold father dead, his glossed eyes
> New closed up by thy sad mother's hands?
> Hast thou a love, as spotless as the brow
> Of clearest heaven, blurr'd with false defames?
> Are thy moist entrails crumpled up with grief
> Of parching mischiefs? Tell me, does thy heart
> With punching anguish spur thy galled ribs?
> Then come, and let's sit and weep and wreathe
> our arms;
> I'll hear thy counsel.
> Alberto Take comfort.
> Antonio Confusion to all comfort! I defy it.
> Comfort's a parasite, a flatt'ring Jack,
> And melts resolv'd despair.
> (*AR*, I. ii. 269–86)

Similarly he later rejects Senecan philosophy to 'endure bravely': 'Pish, thy mother was not lately widowed, / Thy dear affied love lately defam'd' (*AR*, II. ii. 50–1). And, finally, despite his promise to Mellida that he 'will not swell like a tragedian' (*AR*, II. ii. 105), after only a few more words he is prostrate on the ground again, crying out 'player-like',

> Behold a prostrate wretch laid on his tomb;
> His epitaph thus: *Ne plus ultra*. Ho!
> Let none out-woe me; mine's Herculean woe.
> (*AR*, II. ii. 132–4)

Thus we see a consistency in Antonio's presentation of emotional instability from *Antonio and Mellida* and it is this which is to cause his destruction. By continually abandoning rational comfort and submission so as to indulge in the extremities of emotion, Antonio becomes mentally sick. His sanguine humour predominates –

> Methinks I am all air and feel no weight
> Of human dirt clog
>
> (*AR*, III, ii. 82–3)

> Then will I dance and whirl about the air.
> Methinks I am all soul, all heart, all spirit
>
> (*AR*, V. iii. 47–8)[16]

– and his mother fears for his sanity: 'What, my good boy, stark mad?' (*AR*, II. ii. 145).

It is in this vulnerable state that in Act III, scene i, Antonio enters St Mark's Church to celebrate 'due obsequies' over his father's tomb. Professor Hunter has recognised that this scene is framed around the celebration of the Requiem Mass.[17] Although accompanied by signs of madness, Antonio's first actions in the church are essentially Christian. He lights candles and swings a thurible incensing the tomb. On the appearance of the ghost, however, his emotive state and aimless actions are given a definite end and he himself a positive role. He is to become the priest of Vengeance, to whom he solemnly dedicates himself:

> *O quisquis nova*
> *Supplicia functis durus umbrarum arbiter*
> *Disponis, quisquis exeso iaces*
> *Pavidus sub antro, quisquis venturi times*
> *Montis ruinam, quisquis avidorum feros*
> *Rictus leonum, et dira furiarum agmina*
> *Implicitus horres, Antonii vocem excipe*
> *Properantis ad vos: Ulciscar.*
>
> (*AR*, III. i. 66–73)

The link with the Mass is stressed by the use of Latin. The celebrant of this liturgy is Antonio. Although Protestant theology refutes it, Catholic doctrine of the Eucharist Sacrifice has from early times stressed that the priest is an actor playing the role of Christ:

> The priest who celebrates bears in himself the image of our Lord in that hour. All the priests in the sanctuary bear the image of the Apostles who met together at the sepulchre. The altar is a symbol

of our Lord's tomb, and the bread and wine are the Body of the Lord which was embalmed and buried.[18]

Antonio as an actor–priest in his ritual becomes totally associated with his supernatural god-like entity, Vengeance. He speaks as one removed from reality:

By the astoning terror of swart night,
By the infectious damps of clammy graves,
And by the mold that presseth down
My dead father's skull, I'll be revenged!
(*AR*, III. i. 76–9)

Revenge need not be present on stage, as in *The Spanish Tragedy*, since within his black ritual Antonio becomes fully identifiable with Vengeance. The audience is captivated by the action and the atmosphere. We must remember that the play was written for the confines of a private theatre, probably annexed to St Paul's, where spectators would have been very near to the action – close enough to smell the burning incense. The incantations of the protagonist continues in their rhythm. The priest dwells on the imagery of disease, death and vengeance. The emotive power is increased by the tripartite command heard from various parts of the church.

Andrugio Murder!
Feliche Murder! [*From above and beneath.*]
Pandulpho Murder!
(*AR*, III. i. 125–7)

'Sanctus, Sanctus, Sanctus', but within this ritual where is the sacrificial victim to be found? As with Abraham and Isaac the supernatural provides the lamb, but in this perverted rite there is to be no reprieve for the innocent. Julio has entered, babbling about his father:

Antonio Thy father! Gracious, O bounteous heaven!
I do adore thy justice: *venit in nostras manus*
Tandem vindicta, venit et tota quidem.
(*AR*, III. i. 150–2)

The language is again Latin, which is important, since the tension and atmosphere must be sustained to the point of sacrifice or consecration. Like an altar boy not understanding his words, Julio answers the Antonio chants:

'Truth, since my mother died I lov'd you best.
Something hath anger'd you; pray you, look merrily.
(*AR*, III. i. 153–4)

His remarks have a dramatic innocence within them:

O God, you'll hurt me. For my sister's sake,
Pray you do not hurt me. And you kill me, 'deed,
I'll tell my father.
(*AR*, III. i. 170–2)

Although this statement of pure innocence has an initial effect over the protagonist he is encouraged by the ghost's command of 'Revenge' to continue in the rite. He becomes more and more intoxicated with the thought of the act he is to perform. Rationality becomes inverted totally as madness twists logic:

It is not thee I hate, not thee I kill.
Thy father's blood that flows within thy veins
It is I loathe, is that revenge must suck.
I love thy soul, and were my heart lapp'd up
In any flesh but in Piero's blood
I would thus kiss it. . . .
(*AR*, III. i. 178–83)

Such a breakdown in reason prevents him from noticing Julio's next dramatically affecting remark: 'So you will love me, do even what you will' (*AR*, III. i. 186). Rather he goes into his elevated incantation

Now barks the wolf against the full cheek'd moon,
Now lions' half-clamm'd entrails roar for food,
Now croaks the toad and night-crows screech aloud,
Fluttering 'bout casements of departing souls;
Now gapes the graves, and through their yawns let loose
Imprison'd spirits to revisit earth;
And now, swart night, to swell thy hour out,
Behold I spurt warm blood in thy black eyes.
[*Stabs* Julio.]
(*AR*. III. i. 187–94)

This killing sees the actor–priest in the frenzy of intoxication and animal lust.[19] It has sexual overtones in its climactic quality, but the spirit of vengeance is not fully ejaculated by Antonio. Rather the killing only intensifies his passion. The priest becomes blood-mad:

Lo, thus I heave my blood-dyed hands to heaven;
Even like insatiate hell, still crying: 'More!
My heart hath thirsting dropsies after gore.'
(*AR*, III. i. 211–13)

Antonio having totally lost self-control is as completely possessed by Vengeance as the priest–dancer in pagan ritual – so much so, indeed, that the ghost is forced to intervene to prevent him from murdering his mother, and to make him regain his reason by acting out another role:

Pardon ignorance.
Fly, dear Antonio.
Once more assume disguise, and dog the court
In feigned habit till Piero's blood
May even o'erflow the brim of full revenge.
(*AR*. III. ii. 85–9)

The instructions are doubly ironic. First, the ghost is being forced, by the circumstances of Antonio's enthusiasm, to direct the revenger to resort to rational conduct in order to execute a passionate desire for vengeance. Secondly, Andrugio, by allowing Antonio to assume the rational act, is paradoxically giving him the opportunity to save himself from his unregulated passion. In the context of the relationship between the actor and his role Antonio reaches a critical stage. Is his act to be based on the essential rational or irrational parts of his nature? The character he now assumes is that of the fool, not the madman. It is the fool that is totally rational:

note a fool's beatitude:
He is not capable of passion;
Wanting the power of distinction,
He bears an unturn'd sail with every wind;
Blow east, blow west, he stirs his course alike.
(*AR*, IV. i. 38–42)

In assuming this role Antonio is to have his last chance of releasing himself from his sanguine humour and his possession by Vengeance. Just as he became identified with Vengeance itself when he acted the role of sacrificial priest, so now, in adopting the persona of the fool, incapable of passion, Antonio may become identified with the motley and save himself from irrationality.

Perhaps it is because he is unable to 'recall' the experience of such mechanical reasoning that this new role fails. At first all does go well, but no one tells Mellida of Antonio's new act nor of the plan to report his 'death'. The result is that, on hearing the account given to Piero, she dies of grief. Her death is of utmost significance, for it thrusts Antonio back into his extremes of passion and inspires him to rededicate himself to Vengeance. He enters alone, casts off the fool's cap, deliberately lies on his back and prays to the heavens:

> Look here, behold!
> I turn my prostrate breast upon thy face,
> And vent a heaving sigh. O hear but this:
> I am a poor, poor orphan; a weak, weak child,
> The wrack of splitted fortune, the very ooze,
> The quicksand that devours all misery.
> Behold the valiant'st creature that doth breathe!
> For all this, I dare live, and I will live,
> Only to numb some others' cursed blood
> With the dead palsy of like misery.
> Then death, like to a stifling Incubus,
> Lie on my bosom. Lo, sir, I am sped.
> My breast is Golgotha, grave for the dead.
> (*AR*, IV. ii. 11–23)

It is here that Pandulpho enters and symbolically marries Antonio with death by laying Feliche's body across his breast. Antonio is recommitted to his final action of revenge.

The progression towards the final act of purification by murder is again ritually climactic in presentation. The murderers slide into the rhythm of incantation:

> Antonio Scum of the mud of hell!
> Alberto Slime of all filth!
> Maria Thou most detested toad!
> Balurdo Thou most retort and obtuse rascal!
> Antonio Thus charge we death at thee. Remember hell;
> And let the howling murmurs of black spirits,
> The horrid torments of the damned ghosts,
> Affright thy soul as it descendeth down
> Into the entrails of the ugly deep.
> Pandulpho Sa, sa; no, let him die and die, and still be dying
>
> *They offer to run all at* Piero, *and on a sudden stop*.
>
> And yet not die till he hath died and died
> Ten thousand deaths in agony of heart.
> Antonio Now, pell-mell! Thus the hand of heaven chokes
> The throat of murder. This for my father's blood!
> [*He stabs* Piero.]

Pandulpho	This for my son! [*Stabs.*]
Alberto	This for them all! [*Stabs.*]
	And this, and this! Sink to the heart of hell!

They all run at Piero *with their rapiers.*

(*AR*, v. iii. 96–112)

Again Antonio is shown to be dominated by his humour. Just prior to the assassination he mutters in expectation:

Methinks I am all soul, all heart, all spirit.
Now murder shall receive his ample merit.
(*AR*, v. iii. 48–9)

The murder itself in its intensity and its similarity with that of Julio's shows him as a man possessed. Indeed, he gives adequate proof of this when in answer to a statement he illustrates that he has lost sight of the true reason for his deed:

Second Senator	Alas, poor orphan!
Antonio	Poor?
	Standing triumphant over Belzebub?
	Having large interest for blood; and yet deem'd poor?

(*AR*, v. iii. 137–9)

This statement, however, brings us to a final problem in the play: its incongruous conclusion. Throughout, Antonio, like Pandulpho and Piero, has become an actor – albeit, unlike their deceptions, his act has been a subconscious one. Instead of employing reason as a disguise for his passionate nature, he has totally divorced himself from his reason and has allowed himself to wallow in the obscenities of revenge, becoming its pawn. In the light of this horrific fact the prize which he receives in the conclusion of the play is hard to reconcile with what has gone before. Piero dead, Pandulpho and Antonio argue before the senators for the glory of the deed. Their actions have been so horrific that we, as audience, might well expect the senators to condemn them; but no, the Second Senator pronounces judgement,

Bless'd be you all; and may your honors live,
Religiously held sacred, even for ever and ever.
(*AR*, v. iii. 127–8)

This statement at first shocks us and our immediate reaction is to reject it, but on reflection it may be seen as a fitting end to all that has preceded it. Philip Ayres instructively notes,

> What Marston does in the remainder of his play is to undermine the sympathetic attitude he has encouraged by working out a number of situations that involve his audience in an understanding of the real nature of the revenger. The process reaches its climax in the final scene, where Marston ridicules the myth of the heroic revenger by emphasizing it and at the same time highlighting the paradoxes it involves – to such an extent that the survival of the heroes is received with the horror it deserves.[20]

The incongruity is due to the employment of a deliberate dramatic technique which is not merely used on this one occasion but which shows itself throughout both *Antonio* plays. In particular it is employed in the parallel scene (v. ii) in *Antonio and Mellida*. If we look back to our discussion of Piero's character it is apparent that the problems set by the *Antonio and Mellida* conversion scene can be solved by our knowledge of *Antonio's Revenge*. But they are also relieved by understanding the scene in the context of the total dramatic structure being employed. The major problems with *Antonio and Mellida*, Act v, scene ii, lie in Piero's sudden change of heart, just as in *Antonio's Revenge* it is caused by the senators' rather startling judgement. In the former play, as we have seen, Piero, on realising the valour of Andrugio, represses his emotion and, as far as the audience of that work alone is immediately concerned, reforms his character. His words are regal in their formality and control:

> We are amaz'd, our royal spirits numb'd
> In stiff astonish'd wonder at thy prowess,
> Most mighty, valiant and high-tow'ring heart.
> We blush, and turn our hate upon ourselves
> For hating such an unpeer'd excellence.
> I joy my state, him whom I loath'd before
> That now I honor, love, nay more, adore.
> (*A & M*, v. ii. 166–72)

In the context of Marston's satiric attitude throughout the plays in building up and then breaking down a character's emotion, we might, as Hunter suggests,[21] be able to justify the reformation; as with other episodes in the play we are seeing one attitude suddenly juxtaposed with another. Nevertheless, even if we allow ourselves to accept Piero's statements as being honest words testifying to a new-found charity, we should at the same time be wrong to regard them as having an enduring quality or even hinting at a permanent situation. Nothing in the play has indicated that such immutable states of emotion or rationality could exist. The game which Marston has been playing throughout has illustrated, by the contradictory portrayals of excessive emotion or dramatic poses, the complete yet transitory effect and validity of a moment's excitement or depression: one minute a man can be extremely happy without any troubles, whilst the next he can be in the depths of despair. Each instantaneous emotion at its time of occurrence, however, has been a true one for the individual concerned: the actor becoming his act, the emotional man becoming his emotion. The audience has been made aware of the frailty of each state by Marston's repeated satiric method. The result is that nothing can be permanently believed in this world of make-believe, for nothing has the quality of endurance. That Piero's speech is incongruous with the nature he has presented in the play should, in fact, be enough to set us on our guard and to help us realise the grim significance of Antonio's final words:

> Here ends the comic crosses of true love;
> O may the passage most successful prove.
> (*A & M*, v. ii. 264–5)

It is a vain hope. The sequel is to illustrate that the next crosses are to be tragic.[22] The problem of the senators' judgement on the revengers' butchery in *Antonio's Revenge* is answered in a similar manner. The difficulty here is intensified slightly, since it consists not merely in the fact that, unlike Hieronimo, Titus, Hoffman, Vindice or Hamlet, Antonio fails to meet his own death and, rather, is praised by the Second Senator, but also in that Antonio and his companions suddenly confess their vows to accept a strictly Christian way of life:

> We know the world; and did we know no more
> We would not live to know; but since constraint
> Of holy bands forceth us keep this lodge
> Of dirt's corruption till dread power calls
> Our soul's appearance, we will live enclos'd
> In holy verge of some religious order,
> Most constant votaries.
> (*AR*, v. iii. 147–153)

In view of all that has preceded this statement, it appears discordant, to say the least. That Antonio feels guilt is strange; that he has ever had the rational stability to make a vow is yet stranger; that he and Pandulpho have accepted a traditional morality is strangest of all. Nevertheless, it seems that, for his dramatic aim to be realised, Marston wanted us to feel uneasy with the conclusion.

In the first place it is important to realise that the senators who meet Antonio and his companions are the new rulers of the same world as has been presented to us in the previous action: a world of actors and disguise, of emotional extremes and barbarity, of viciousness and the primitive justice of revenge.[23] In the savage and amoral terms of such a world the revengers' actions are indeed notable. There would have existed a greater incongruity in fact if, during their meeting with them, Antonio and his companions had found the senators to possess a Christian morality. Nevertheless, the incongruity still exists, but it is one based not on the Venice of the play, but upon the moral philosophy of the audience. Throughout, the inversion of Christian values and rites has implicitly reminded us of the moral values of the religion, with the result that our subjective view of morality has been awaiting some form of Christian conclusion, or, at the very least, has expected the immorality of the tyrant and that of the revengers to cancel each other out. That Marston frustrates this shows his brave originality. He attacks the complacency of the audience by presenting not the moral nobleman of *The Revengers' Tragedy* but the corrupt judges of Jonson's *Volpone*.[24] In their acts of 'respectability' the senators of *Antonio's Revenge* are as misguided and amoral as Piero, Pandulpho or Antonio. Marston refuses to allow us to leave the theatre thinking that this is now the best of all possible worlds, for this would make nonsense of the vision that he has presented throughout both plays:

> Galeatzo Well, and what dost thou play?
> Balurdo The part of all the world.
> Alberto The part of all the world? What's that?
> Balurdo The fool.
>
> (*A & M*, Induction, 28–31)

Similarly, the second difficulty, that of the monastic intention, may be resolved by considering the dramatic structure. G. K. Hunter again helps to elucidate the problem:

> Given the reality of the world – 'this lodge of dirt's corruption' – suicide would be (says Pandulpho) the natural conclusion to the action, but under Christianity this is not possible, and monastic retreat until death is the only alternative way of dissociating the soul from the world.[25]

As Hunter notes elsewhere, 'the monastery is a complex image'[26] but one suited to the conduct of the play. Through it we realise that

Marston, after disappointing the moral expectations of his audience by refusing to pander to their conventional attitudes, then characteristically appeals to the very moral positions which he has just deflated. The world is evil, and, in terms of the subjective morality of the audience, the revengers are immoral. To confirm this the dramatist allows the revengers to adopt the subjective morality of the audience. Thus arises the dramatic incongruity in characterisation but one which he attempts to solve by the monastic image, since such an institution will encompass those characteristics of the revengers which have been displayed throughout. Pandulpho will be able to find another philosophical act and this time perhaps one which he will be capable of sustaining, since he will be isolated from the heartbreak of the world. There too, Antonio will be able to dissociate his 'soul from the world', to live a spiritual life with the priests of God and find contentment for his irrational nature. The image therefore is a correct one pandering to those weaknesses, those retreats into rational disguises or emotional absurdities in which Marston's actors have indulged. It is poignant also in emphasising by contrast the immorality of the make-believe world of the *Antonio* plays. Where perhaps it continues to present difficulties is in that, like the attitude of the senators, it refuses to allow the play to achieve an aesthetic unity – a fact which must have disturbed all who saw the play performed. However, in deliberately designing such a frustration, Marston ends the play characteristically by laughing at his audience. He has broken the artistic rules in order to project a new look at traditional moral positions. This in terms of the audience's presumptions is not what he was expected to have done, so he prays that, if ever anyone should write the tragic story of *Antonio and Mellida*, they should do it with the professionalism and insight of the traditional artist:

> And, O, if ever time create a muse
> That to th' immortal fame of virgin faith
> Dares once engage his pen to write her death,
> Presenting it in some black tragedy,
> May it prove gracious, may his style be deck'd
> With freshest blooms of purest elegance;
> May it have gentle presence, and the scenes suck'd up
> By calm attention of choice audience;
> And when the closing Epilogue appears,
> Instead of claps may it obtain but tears.
>
> (*AR*, v. iii. 177–86)

His final ironic cynicism is at our expense.

3
Absurdities and Illusions

If John Webster's Induction to *The Malcontent* is any indication, it seems that early Jacobean audiences may have been perplexed by what has become Marston's best-known work. The critical problem that has concerned *The Malcontent* since it was first performed is argued out by two actors, Sly and Condell:

Sly	Do you hear, sir, this play is a bitter play?
Condell	Why, sir, 'tis neither satire nor moral, but the mean passage of a history; yet there are a sort of discontented creatures that bear a stingless envy to great ones, and these will wrest the doings of any man to their base malicious applyment; but should their interpretation come to the test, like your marmoset they presently turn their teeth to their tail and eat it.
Sly	I will not go so far with you; but I say, any man that hath wit may censure – if he sit in the twelve penny room – and I say again, the play is bitter.

(Induction to *The Malcontent*, 51–61)[1]

Many men of 'wit' have taken Sly at his word and censured the work, seeing in it an apparent disharmony in characterisation, structure and tone. They have claimed further that the problems and issues the play raises are incompatible with the levity found in the tragicomic form throughout and in the conclusion in particular.[2] Such criticism, however, seems to have neglected the value of Sly's judgement. The play is 'bitter'; that does not mean to say it is not comic, but rather it implies that the humour contains a cynicism which is only too pertinent. Thinking in these terms, Hunter has offset some of the criticism by illustrating how Marston employed the 'tragicomic form' in a unique way so as to provide 'an excellent theatrical vehicle for the satiric impulse';[3] an impulse which, as a number of critics have noted, seems strangely relevant to the twentieth-century audiences acquainted with, for example, French *avant-garde* writers.[4] Genet's tantalising cruelty, Sartre's hell, Beckett's despair, Artaud's sadism often appear to be anticipated by the Jacobean in both technique and philosophy. Genet's *The Balcony* in particular comes to mind when we examine *The Malcontent*, especially in its complex relationship of game with reality. Madame Irma's brothel entertains faceless characters: bishop, judge, or general revelling in a perverse authority which is both political and sexual. The image presented is of a grotesque sport in which reality becomes an irrelevance to characters who indulge in obscene fantasy. We even find a faceless individual masochistically enjoying filth. The people behind the mask are never shown to us, since their façade is more real than their everyday existence, the metaphor of Genet's brothel being the exposition of an obscene reality. We see this also with Marston. Critics have argued over and over again about the role of the malcontent.[5] Is Altofront merely acting a part in his disguise or is he really as obscene as Malevole? The answer, as we shall see, is that both Altofront and Malevole are disguises of a faceless individual living in a court that revels in role-play, hypocrisy and perversion. The character who plays deposed duke and malcontent is merely one of a number taking on similar roles. Two of these, Pietro and Mendoza, assume, at one time or another, the persona of prince playing a similar game of authority as opposed to a former role of subservience. This creation of dramatic caricature and role-play rather than character delineation allows Marston (as it does Genet) to express his own cynical vision of society through a dramatic metaphor. The world of authority is drawn in terms of a political brothel and house of illusions.

The preoccupation with the idea of role-play begins, as T. F. Wharton states, before the start of the first act:

> It is no accident that the Induction Webster wrote for its Globe presentation plays such obvious games with the idea of actor and audience (some of the actors appearing in their own persons to discuss the play with other actors disguised as spectators). The Induction here faithfully reflects the play, whose concluding masque is performed by courtiers impersonating actors.[6]

The Induction over, however, we hear 'the vilest out-of-tune music' (stage direction) and see the entrance of a 'choleric old marshall' and an effeminate usher calling for silence. Hunter notes that this is a technically effective way of silencing the audience and starting the play.[7] But, more important, Bilioso's and Prepasso's entrance signifies an immediate attempt to relate the fantasy of dramatic action to the reality of the audience:

> Bilioso   Here's a noise in court! you think you are in a tavern, do you not?
>
> Prepasso   You think you are in a brothel-house, do you not? This room is ill scented. So, perfume, perfume; some upon

> me, I pray thee. The Duke is upon instant entrance: so make place there.
>
> (*The Malcontent*, I. i. 4–9)

Of course, taverns, brothels and theatres to many were pretty much the same thing. Prepasso and Bilioso are therefore asking for a licence of fantasy. This brothel-house of the theatre is to become the duke of Genoa's court, but unfortunately the Genoese world, in being emblematic of a real palace, is a little like a brothel-house and quite similar to a theatre. So, just as in a performance a façade must be laid, Prepasso immediately calls for perfume. The court will disguise putrefaction with scent, barbarism with shallow civilisation, and disorder with the order of game. For, in the world which the play is to portray, 'your whore went down with the stews, and your punk came up with your puritan' (V. iv. 33–4). Hypocrisy is the rule of the game. The point is driven home further by the entrance of the euphuistic duke: 'Where breathes that music?' he asks. There is no music, only Malevole's cacophony; but if we pretend long enough the malcontent's discord will become harmony, his obscenities philosophy, and evil the measure of respectability. Sin will disappear as it does in Genet's brothel, where the bishop tells the bawd, 'Here there's no possibility of doing evil. You live in evil. In the absence of remorse. How could you do evil? The Devil makes believe. That's how one recognises him. He's the great Actor.'[8] This is exactly how we recognise him in Genoa. The great actor of Pietro's court as the duke tells us himself, is Malevole: 'one of the most prodigious affections that ever conversed with nature, a man, or rather a monster, more discontent than Lucifer when he was thrust out of the presence' (I. ii. 17). More malcontented than the devil himself the protagonist wanders the court moaning his fall from power and brooding on its cause:

> Behold forever-banished Altofront,
> This Genoa's last year's Duke. O truly noble!
> I wanted those old instruments of state,
> Dissemblance and Suspect: I could not time it, Celso;
> My throne stood like a point in midst of a circle,
> To all of equal nearness, bore with none,
> Reigned all alike, so slept in fearless virtue,
> Suspectless, too suspectless. . . .
>
> (I. iv. 7–14)

In the past it has been thought that this passage portrays the man beneath the act. Here is the worthy duke revealing himself to the audience and to Celso. Yet his language and attitude has a sense of falsehood about it. Why should the protagonist have to show himself with such formality to Celso or remind the 'constant Lord' of the reason for his disposition? Not only are formal apologies and excuses being laid down ('I could not time it'), but pride is also showing itself ('O truly noble!'). The speech in fact shows no passion or emotion, which leads us to suspect that the protagonist has merely altered his persona slightly. By being objective in his commentary on his own character he is describing another fictitious role which he sometimes plays, that of the duke. All that we as an audience are seeing is the shell of the egg, the protective covering of the reality, but obviously there are differences in colour and shape of the shell itself and it is these which Marston has his protagonist describe to us at different times throughout the play. He even tells us that when he was duke his act was not good enough for him to remain in power: 'I wanted those old instruments of state, / Dissemblance and Suspect'. We must, of course, allow for some irony here, but, even so, adopting the role of malcontent he is studying to be a better actor, and what better part to choose than that of a discontent? As Stanislavsky has told us, you cannot act a role unless you have an affinity with it; the part has to be an extension and recollection of feelings already experienced or presently being felt in real life. This is the closest we are able to get to the protagonist's true nature. Philip Finkelpearl has already pointed out the appropriateness of the character's malcontented role: a deposed duke is naturally discontented, since he has been usurped from his position in the divine order of life.[9] Thus it is not in the deposed duke that we should look for the man behind the mask, but in the malcontent. Let us turn to his great soliloquy:

I cannot sleep; my eyes' ill-neighbouring lids
Will hold no fellowship. O thou pale sober night,
Thou that in sluggish fumes all sense dost steep,
Thou that gives all the world full leave to play,
Unbend'st the feebled veins of sweaty labour –
The galley-slave, that all the toilsome day
Tugs at his oar against the stubborn wave,
Straining his rugged veins, snores fast;
The stooping scythe-man, that doth barb the field,
Thou makest wink sure. In night all creatures sleep;
Only the malcontent, that 'gainst his fate
Repines and quarrels – alas, he's goodman tell-clock!
His sallow jaw-bones sink with wasting moan;
Whilst others' beds are down, his pillow's stone.

(III. ii. 1–14)

The speech raises immediate vital questions. What is the relevance of the 'galley-slave' or the 'scythe-man' to this deposed duke? Why should he be so unhappy, since all his plans for regaining the throne are going well? The speech never mentions these and, more important, neither does it emphasise the wrongs that have befallen him. Rather it is an unemotional panegyric to the nature of the malady he would like to feel, but which, due to the lack of passion displayed both here and with Celso, we suspect does not exist. Perhaps when he was in power he was so infatuated with playing the part of the virtuous man that he never really came to terms with the reality of the role. Perhaps, indeed, he never comes to the stark truth of either part, duke or malcontent, that he plays throughout the drama.

It is such questions as these which bring us to the main problem of the play. If the protagonist is really the discontented individual which he pretends, the man who pours scorn down on all about him, would he merely dismiss Mendoza as a fly at the end of the play? Possibly, since earlier he professed that the deepest revenge is the 'heart's disquiet' rather than blood-letting (I. iii. 159–60), but when he reascends the throne, in Act V, scene vi, the protagonist has discarded his act of Malevole. The act of malcontent died when he was poisoned by Mendoza with his own empty box, in Act V, scene iv. From that time on the protagonist is never seen again in the person of Malevole. The people that do accompany him are rather those that have already acknowledged him as Duke Altofront: Celso, Ferneze, Pietro. Thus it is that in sentencing Mendoza the protagonist is firmly back in his role as duke, but the sentence and the speech preceding it emphasise that as duke he is merely assuming a former role. His words and actions are as divorced from reality as any of his earlier language and deeds have been. His pious platitudes, now devoted to a description of the regal nature, are merely an example of the 'outward shows' which he is condemning. They are as irrelevant to the situation as were his moral expletives expressed earlier in the play when Ferneze lay dying. On that occasion (II. v. 146–61) he eventually stopped moralising and tended to the reality of the boy's wounds (156 ff.) but in Act V proud philosophy and regal affectation are his only concerns. Just as in Genet's play bishop, judge and general are, owing to their role-playing, immune to the political actuality of the revolution outside, and yet are by necessity eventually involved in the reality of the situation, so Altofront at the end of Marston's drama is entangled in a political paradox. He is duke and has political responsibilities, one of which is to judge miscreants, but since this shallow individual can only play-act at regality he is impotent in the face of political expediency and judgement. Divorced from the possible danger of the situation, still sleeping in his act of 'fearless virtue' which deposed him before, Altofront merely *kicks out Mendoza*. This is an example of his affectation and self-adulation, and is consequently dangerous, since this role-play negates the possibility of his realising that the 'heart's disquiet' could lead Mendoza to more Machiavellian schemes. Such an idea is an irrelevance to a character whose only interest is to appear as the virtuous king.

Duke, malcontent, Machiavellian, magician, bawd, poet – Altofront plays all the roles and consequently never reveals his essential self. Only once do we gain any possible impression that beneath the act there is a character. This occurs when after visiting his wife in prison he broods, 'O God, how loathesome this toying is to me!' (v. iii. 43), but such an insight, if it is one, is immediately disguised again: 'Well, *stultorum plena sunt omnia*: better play the fool lord than be the fool lord' (44–6). The protagonist, however, is not alone in his acts. All the other characters, with the exception of the minor figures Celso and Maria, are likewise indulging in role-play. Bilioso, the 'muck-hill overspread with snow', Pietro, badly cast and out-played as the new duke, and the other arch dissimulator, Mendoza, all revel in the hypocrisy of Madame Maquerelle's, rather than Madame Irma's, house of illusion. Like Genet, Marston links the political façade and impotence of the ruling class with the sexual activities of the old bawd.[10] In his play Genet draws an anarchic metaphor so as to ridicule both social order and social change as being equally inadequate in the face of an absurd existence. For him 'Man is a tragic joke in a context of total cosmic absurdity.'[11] Marston does not quite go so far, but by creating faceless, obscene caricatures he, like Genet, enabled himself to attack the evil, misconceptions and hypocrisy of the society in which he lived.

In an early satire Marston wrote,

I Cannot hold, I cannot I indure
To view a big womb'd foggie clowde immure
The radiant tresses of the quickning sunne.
Let Custards quake, my rage must freely runne.
Preach not the Stoickes patience to me,
I hate no man, but mens impietie[12]

but in *The Malcontent* he has learnt that the way to expose 'mens impietie' is to draw exaggerations of those very clouds which keep out the sun. The role-playing of the characters is clearly, as we have seen, an essential aspect of his criticism of society. Kingship and the life at court may be as dangerously shallow as these puppets that parade before us on the stage, as obscene as the hypocrisy of love in a brothel. Just to make his point even more clear, however, Marston takes the opportunity of using his hollow malcontent as a mouthpiece for the truth being expressed by the play as a whole. Thus the 'hypocrite' taunts levelled at Bilioso, the 'old coal' descriptions of Maquerelle, the satiric quips as 'honesty and courtship straddle as far asunder as a true Frenchman's legs (II. v. 138–9) and the sometimes vicious verbal attacks on Pietro and Mendoza. More important even than these, however, are the specific statements made in the presence of Pietro. These take two forms. The first are those still seen under the violent disguise of the malcontent. Heavily weighted with mythical, classical or religious allusion they point out the decadence of the court and the pointless absurd irrelevance of it all:

> Here a Paris supports that Helen; there's a Lady Guinever bears up that Sir Lancelot . . . Sir Tristram Trimtram, come aloft Jack-an-apes with a whim wham: here's a Knight of the land of Catito shall play at trap with any page in Europe, do the sword-dance with any morris-dancer in Christendom, ride at the ring till the fin of his eyes look as blue as the welkin, and run the wild goose chase even with Pompey the Huge.
>
> (I. iii. 53–62)

The second however, are those which illustrate the situation in 'plain-tongued' language:

> Think this – this earth is the only grave and Golgotha wherein all things that live must rot; 'tis but the draught wherein the heavenly bodies discharge their corruption; the very muck-hill on which the sublunary orbs cast their excrements. Man is the slime of this dung-pit, and princes are the governors of these men; for, for our souls, they are as free as emperors', all of one piece; there goes but a pair of shears betwixt an emperor and the son of a bagpiper; only the dyeing, dressing, pressing, glossing, makes the difference.
>
> (IV. v. 110–19)

The human body, materialistic society, princely authority are all absurd degradations of the spirit. They are meaningless. This is the philosophy Marston is expounding, but his mastery is seen by the fact that Malevole, in speaking thus, is only attempting to make Pietro renounce regency so that Altofront may regain the throne. It is all part of his act and he doesn't believe a word of it or, if he does, chooses to ignore his own advice. Paradoxically, therefore, the truth is being uttered by the hypocritical. Such a situation, Marston is saying, is the lot of man; and, as though to emphasise the point, the playwright throughout attacks that part of society which is most culpable in the crime, the church:

Pietro	And, sir, whence come you now?
Malevole	From the public place of much dissimulation, the church.

(I. iii. 3–5)

Malevole	Sects, sects; I have seen seeming Piety change her robe so oft, that sure none but some arch-devil can shape her a petticoat.

(I. iii. 11–13)

Malevole	I ha' seen a sumptuous steeple turned to a stinking privy; more beastly, the sacredest place made a dog's kennel; nay, most inhuman, the stoned coffins of long-dead Christians burst up, and made hogs' troughs. . . .

(II. v. 128–31)

Mendoza
Hermit, thou art a man for me, my confessor;
O thou selected spirit, born for my good,
Sure thou wouldst make an excellent Elder
In a deformed church.

(IV. iii. 96–9)

Mendoza
A churchman once corrupted, O, avoid!
A fellow that makes religion his stalking-horse,
He breeds a plague. . . .

(IV. iii. 128–30)

If the church cannot maintain the truth without either hypocrisy or degradation there is perhaps little hope for secular society. At the end of the play Marston reveals that no one, with the possible exception of Aurelia and Pietro, who are almost ignored, has truly learnt from the experience of the game. There has been no purge of folly or evil. Ferneze makes indecent proposals to Bianca; Maquerelle is allowed to continue her school of prostitutes, in the suburbs rather than in the court; Bilioso is affectionately rebuked; Mendoza goes unpunished; the protagonist assumes his old role. The moral is that expressed in *The Balcony*, which ends with preparation for new acts – Irma realising that 'In a little while, I'll have to start all over again . . . put all the lights on again . . . dress up. . . . Dress up . . . ah, the disguises! Distribute roles again . . . assume my own . . .' (*The Balcony*, pp. 95–6). So with *The Malcontent*: 'only the dyeing, dressing, pressing, glossing, makes the difference'. This is the truth of the play, but the bitterness is that none of the characters, though echoing the truth, can see it. At the close we have the distinct impression that the 'goose chase' might very well start again.

Reference to Genet helps to illustrate Marston's strangely modern cynicism and mode of expression. Many of his characters, not only in *The Malcontent* but in all his plays, are portrayed as figures chasing unobtainable ambitions or ideals. As Mendoza says of Ferneze, 'The fool grasps clouds, and shall beget centaurs' (II. i. 4) In twentieth-century drama such situations tend to describe a metaphor of eternal frustration, life becoming a tantalising nightmare: 'You won't catch anything. We're chasing after each other, round and round in a vicious circle, like the horses on a roundabout.'[13] This is Sartre's view, but it is one which has been seen periodically by authors since the earliest times. It is a vision of the total futility of action, Sisyphus rolling his stone, Tantalus grasping for fruit; a nightmare which André Gide finds in all great writers: 'Not one of the great specialists of the human heart, be his name Shakespeare, Cervantes or Racine, has failed to have at any rate fleeting glimpses of the inconsequence of human beings.'[14] Marston was by no means 'a specialist of the human heart', but he did have the vision, which he seemed unable to discard, of absurdity in human action. It became therefore a permanent feature in his dramatic expression. In this respect he is almost unique among the English Renaissance dramatists. Ironically, in the one play, *Sophonisba*, in which he felt confident that he would be able to affirm positive rather than negative values, he succeeds only in drawing his bitter picture of inconsequence in a more depressing manner than in any of his preceding works. Anthony Caputi is slightly misleading in his belief that the play is devoid of Marston's usual cynicism.[15] This may have been the author's avowed intention, in that he wished to replace satire with the adulation of virtue in the wonder of women, but, as will become apparent, although the plot moves towards this design, the theme counters it in illustrating the final impotence of virtue in the face of vice throughout human society.

The characters created in *Sophonisba* are not morally fictitious like Altofront, Mendoza or Maquerelle, but historically as real as Shakespeare's Antony or Jonson's Sejanus. By historical reconstruction Marston's cynicism is being levelled for the first time directly, rather than through metaphor, at mankind. His characters really lived. Yet, as Peter Ure pointed out in his excellent essay on the work,[16] the actual structuring of the character-groups strongly resembles those found in a traditional morality drama. Virtue and Vice are set in opposition, with Massinissa, Sophonisba and Gelosso on the one side, Syphax, Asdrubal and the Carthaginians on the other. Thus, what Marston is doing is rather complex. Whilst taking pagan characters from Livy and Appian, he is placing them in a traditional Christian form of drama, and through the fusion of both he is unwittingly expressing a peculiar dark and pessimistic cynicism.

The story of the lovers placed within the morality structure deceives the audience, for the greater part of the play's action, into thinking that practical politics and honesty can happily co-exist. Massinissa, Gelosso and Sophonisba place their belief in an ethic code of virtue rather than *virtù*. Safety is in the hands of the gods, not the politicians. Thus Sophonisba tells the counsellors,

> 'tis not safe for *Carthage* to destroy,
> Be most unjust, cunninglie politique,
> Your heads still under Heaven, O trust to fate,
> *Gods prosper more a just then crafty state.*
> *Tis lesse disgrace to have a pitied losse,*
> *Then shamefull victory.*
>
> (*Sophonisba*, p. 22)[17]

As events turn out this seems to be sound advice. Gelosso's honesty enables him to warn Massinissa of his danger; Massinissa's virtue startles Gisco to such an extent as to restrain him from his murderous task; Sophonisba's purity amazes Syphax so as to prevent him from raping her; and finally Massinissa triumphs in arms over Syphax because 'angels waite / Upon good harts' (p. 55).

In contrast, the vicious find only frustration and humiliation in their deeds. Asdrubal's policy that 'The God of wisemen is themselves, not lucke' (p. 28) results in his city's defeat by Scipio, his own death by poison and the degradation of having his body thrown to the wild animals. His ghost warns, 'Mortals O feare to sleight / Your Gods and vowes: *Joves* arme is of dread might' (p. 53). Similarly, Syphax is only tantalised by his deeds. Although he allows Sophonisba her freedom, he still lusts after her – to such an extent as to sleep with a diabolic image of her body. He awakes to discover the frustration of carnal sensuality:

> Thou rotten scum of Hell –
> O my abhorred heat! O loath'd delusion!
> . . .
> Can we yet breathe? Is any plagued like me?
> . . . thou, gay God of riddles and strange tales
> Hot-brained *Phebus*, all adde if you can
> Something unto my misery. . . .
>
> (pp. 51–2)

The god of vice is the deity of illusion, riddles and frustration. Follow him and you court disaster. This certainly seems to be the moral behind the dramatic events. Quite suddenly, however, all changes at the moment when virtue seems to be unassailable. When Massinissa defeats Syphax and holds him at his mercy, Marston, having to fuse his morality structure with the Roman story, is forced to introduce a bitter irony. Massinissa demands of Syphax, 'Lives *Sophonisba* yet unstaind, speak just; / Yet ours unforcd?' (p. 55). Syphax affirms that she does and is consequently allowed to live, Massinissa saying, 'Rise, rise, cease strife, / Heare a most deepe revenge, from us take life' (p. 55). The implication is clear. If Sophonisba had been abused Syphax would have died. But, as it is, Massinissa has no just cause to execute his enemy. The virtue in Sophonisba which previously had amazed Syphax to restraint now in Massinissa prevents him from destroying his enemy. It dictates that mercy must be shown since, as he earlier held, 'The God-like part of Kings is to forgive' (p. 26). Virtue is unable to destroy vice without becoming vicious itself. Syphax, freed by the virtuous, is able to win his first – but, ironically, the final and most important – victory in the drama. Quite simply, he achieves this by compromising Massinissa's own code of ethics. At one and the same time Massinissa finds himself vowed to allow Sophonisba her freedom and to obey Scipio's orders, which are to deliver the princess to Roman bondage. The audience discovers that there is no human answer to virtue set at variance with itself. Massinissa cries out, 'which way / Runne mad impossible distraction' (p. 60). The only solution is death, which Sophonisba, Christ-like, takes and so releases virtue from vicious bondage on earth:

> O my stars,
> I blesse your goodnes, that with breast unstaind,
> Faith pure: a Virgin wife, try'de to my glory,
> I die of female faith, the long liv'de story,
> Secure from bondage, and all servile harmes,
> But more, most happy in my husbands armes.
> (p. 61)

It is really impossible to believe that the wonder of women dies 'most happy'. The play has been debating the practice of an ethical code in a political world and has been suggesting the anti-Machiavellian view[18] that there need be no contradiction between moral and political virtue. Marston's Sophonisba placed all her faith in such a philosophy and is consequently led to her death. Thus the dramatist tells us that there is no place for permanent virtue on earth. But why, we must ask, does he allow Massinissa to live? Obviously, in terms of the historical story Massinissa need not die. He in fact lived to an age of about ninety, but in the context of Marston's moral preoccupations in the play Massinissa is not virtuous enough to die. Overtly on the side of virtue throughout, he still falls short of perfection on a number of occasions. First, although in the practical world of arms and politics he was correct to change his allegiance and follow Scipio when he discovered the Carthaginian treachery, morally he sinned against a Stoic code which advocated the turning of the cheek. Secondly, by making oaths which he could not guarantee to Scipio and to Sophonisba, he abused his own sense of honesty and consequently weakened a link in his moral armour. Like Lancelot and Gawain in the old romances he proved to be only too human.

The bitter message of the play rests in the Massylian King's conduct and in Sophonisba's death. Virtue is proved to be an abstraction which negates a positive view to politics. It is an ideal unobtainable on earth and as such an illusion for the characters of the play. For the vicious too the temptations of sex and power are seen to be equally illusory and frustrating. The play ends with both Syphax and Massinissa grieving, but it is the latter's tragedy which conveys the brunt of Marston's black vision. He stands alone with the corpse of his Sophonisba, Stoic in grief:

> Rest all my honour: O thou for whom I drinke
> So deepe of greefe, that he must onely thinke,
> Not dare to speake, that would expresse my woe.
>
> (p. 63)

For the vicious and the virtuous, Marston's world of illusions is indeed a bitter place.

4
Romance or Reality?

If Marston failed to expound fully his aim in *Sophonisba*, at least he was able to keep the dramatic activity as a dominant partner in a theme–structure relationship. Although in the conclusion our sympathies are with Massinissa and our thoughts on the cruel picture Marston has drawn, we do acknowledge that Sophonisba followed a Neo-Platonic code of love, which emphasises that reason and necessity are superior to sensual indulgence. This she first expressed in Act I when she sent Massinissa from the marriage bed to the call of war:

> I entreat
> That you'le collect from our loose form'd speach
> This firme resolve: that no loe Appetite
> Of my sex weakenes, can or shall orecome
> Due gratefull service unto you, or virtue.
> (*Sophonisba*, p. 16)

In this respect *Sophonisba* is technically more successful, although critically less exciting, than Marston's earlier dramatic love debate found in *The Dutch Courtesan*. This play is perhaps Marston's most adventurous. Far from being 'the deliquescence of his talent, and the loss of hard-won ground'[1] *The Dutch Courtesan* illustrates the dramatist's attempts to harmonise a serious philosophic theme within a comic form. Though brave, the experiment fails for two reasons. First, the source-material for the play and its theme is so disparate that it demands an impossible mixture of romance and reality in the plot structure. Secondly, the philosophy proposed, which is mainly derived from two of these same sources, is in itself weak and suspect.

The *Fabulae Argumentum* opens the printed text of the drama with the statement, *'The difference betwixt the love of a courtesan and a wife is the full scope of the play, which, intermixed with the deceits of a witty city jester, fills up the comedy.'*[2] This implies that the play is to examine the Neo-Platonic distinction between sensual indulgence and the true comprehension of beauty, as expressed for example in Book IV of Castiglione's *The Book of the Courtier*.[3] Such a debate on stage could easily be contained in a morality-type play calling for representational figures similar to those employed in *Sophonisba* – Erictho and bestiality, Sophonisba and purity, Syphax and sexuality, Massinissa and Stoicism. This convention, however, is immediately denied to the dramatist, since the Neo-Platonic debate is not his only concern. Not content to rely on Castiglione, Marston chose to employ more heavily the radical *Essayes* of Montaigne.[4] The debt has been shown on many occasions and is well illustrated in Martin Wine's edition of the play. What has not been made clear enough, however, is that Montaigne's philosophy is morally inadequate in that it gives the impression of being totally male-biased. Of all the essays, the one to which Marston is most notably indebted is 'Upon Some Verses of Virgil', in which Montaigne sees love as a distinct entity separated from marriage:

> Wedlocke hath for his share honour, justice, profit and constancie: a plaine, but more generall delight. Love melts in onely pleasure; and truly it hath it more ticklish; more lively, more quaint, and more sharpe: a pleasure inflamed by difficulty: there must be a kinde of stinging, tingling and smarting. *It is no longer love, be it once without Arrowes, or without fire.*
>
> (*Essayes*, Bk III, ch. V.)

Marriage therefore is devoted to social concerns and attributes whereas 'love' divorced from such generalities relies on the sex game. As such, love, like death, becomes the great leveller:

> Nature in mockery left us the most troublesome of our actions, the most common: thereby to equall us, and without distinction to set the foolish and the wise, us and beasts all in one ranke: no barrell better Hering.
>
> (Ibid.)

It is here that the social dilemma of the philosophy becomes apparent. Love is divorced from marriage and yet is a necessary passion. It must be expressed, therefore, outside the married state:

> there hath beene a nation found, which to allay and coole the lustfull concupiscence of such as came for devotion, kept wenches of purpose in their temples to be used; and it was a point of religion to deale with them before one went to prayers. *Nimirum propter continentiam incontinentia necessaria est, incendium ignibus extinguitur. Belike we must be incontinent that we may be continent, burning is quenched by fire.*
>
> (Ibid.)

We might suppose, therefore, that the philosopher is advocating sexual freedom for all, especially as he states that 'both male and female are cast in one same moulde'; but no, sensual liberty is humorously seen as a male prerogative. Wives must be chaste:

> Let us confesse the truth, there are few amongst us, that feare not more the shame they may have by their wives offences, then by their owne vices; or that cares not more (oh wondrous charity) for his wives, then his own conscience; or that had not rather be a theefe and church-robber, and have his wife a murderer and an heretike, then not more chaste then himselfe.
>
> (Ibid.)

A realistic attitude, perhaps, but one which implies a harsh sentence for the sensually active female. The logical result of this thinking is that she, together with the prostitute, 'the wench in the temple', becomes a social outcast. The prostitute, for example, allowing herself sexual freedom to relieve her poverty, is condemned for the very sin which is not only permissible for the man but actually advised for his contentment by the philosopher. Montaigne ignores the problem, but once his thoughts are transferred to a realistic drama the plight of the whore becomes apparent. As we shall see, Marston, in Franceschina, is forced, according to the needs of other sources, to produce a realistic character and so expose the inadequacies of the philosophy which he and Montaigne are proposing.

Whereas Neo-Platonism and Montaigne form the bases of the thematic material in the work, the main plot, as John O'Connor discovered in 1957, relies on Nicholas de Montreux's *Le premier livre des bergeries de Julliette*. In this romance, a whore, Cinthye, deserts her profession when she falls in love with a gallant, Dellio. He loves her for a while but, deciding to marry the more socially acceptable Angelicque, relinquishes his interest in Cinthye, giving her to his friend. The whore plots a revenge but is foiled.[5] Superficially, this seems a reasonable enough plot to accommodate the thematic concerns. Once in practice, however, it proves to contain hidden difficulties. In the Marston play Dellio becomes Freevill, and his friend, Malheureux. But it is with the creation of Malheureux's character that we first encounter serious problems. Depicted as the 'man of snow', he is shown to be foolish enough at first to ignore and neglect his natural sensuality, and then, once he has found 'love', to be unable to make the Platonic distinction between sexual desire and rational beauty. It is in this latter aspect that the author begins to find conflicts between the needs of his plot and his theme. Malheureux, in entering the brothel which he has vehemently condemned, has to be overcome by the enchanting beauty of a whore. But the Neo-

Platonic stance which is to be so central to later developments in the play's morality holds that 'very seldom [doth] an ill soule dwell in a beautifull bodie'.[6] The prostitute therefore has at one and the same time to appear beautiful enough to tempt Malheureux and to convince the audience of the temptation, and yet ugly enough to persuade us of the truth in the Neo-Platonic dictum. A usual Renaissance convention to isolate evil on stage was to present the character as being physically deformed: we think of Richard III or De Flores, which would be in keeping with the Neo-Platonic view, but this technique clearly was not available to Marston with Franceschina. Instead, therefore, he provides her with linguistic deformities, not only by the employment of her Dutch accent, but also by her constant use of profanity. Thus she can appear to be beautiful but be symbolically wrenched from her community by her speech:

> Grand grincome on your sentences! God's sacrament ten tousand devils take you! You ha' brought mine love, mine honor, mine body, all to noting!
>
> (*The Dutch Courtesan*, II. ii. 6–8)[7]

With both the foreign accent and bad language, however, Marston had to be wary that this successful technique did not fall from humour to absurdity, since the courtesan has still to be portrayed seriously enough to attract Malheureux. Thus he is forced to give a reason why such a beauty had fallen. When Castiglione's Bembo explained a similar situation in *The Book of the Courtier*, he cited social depravation and male insensitivity as the principal factors:

> I will not now deny, but it is possible also to finde in the world beautifull women unchaste, yet not because beautie inclineth them to unchaste living, for it rather plucketh them from it, and leadeth them into the way of vertuous conditions, through the affinitie that beautie hath with goodnesse.
>
> But otherwhile ill bringing up, the continuall provocations of lovers, tokens, povertie, hope, deceites, feare, and a thousand other matters overcome the stedfastnesse, yea of beautifull and good women. . . .
>
> (*The Book of the Courtier*, p. 311)

Marston as much as he can follows this line of thought, but in doing so he is in danger of a conflict with the Montaigne source, which advocates total sexual licence to the male, at the expense of the female. For Marston, therefore, male insensitivity has to be extracted from the explanation so that Freevill cannot be blamed for Franceschina's fall. Dramatically this is achieved by the author having Freevill, of all people, tell us that a prostitute's fall is due to social depravation alone, and just in case we might question his morality he frames his speech in comic form:

> Everyman must follow his trade, and every woman her occupation. A poor, decayed mechanical man's wife, her husband is laid up; may not she lawfully be laid down when her husband's only rising is by his wife's falling? A captain's wife wants means, her commander lies in open field abroad; may not she lie in civil arms at home? A waiting gentlewoman, that had wont to take say to her lady, miscarries or so; the court misfortune throws her down; may not the city courtesy take her up? Do you know no alderman would pity such a woman's case? Why is charity grown a sin? or relieving the poor and impotent an offense?
>
> (*The Dutch Courtesan*, I. i. 94–105)

The male's exploitation of the prostitute becomes an act of charity which is seriously proposed beneath the comic façade.

The laughter continues, but Malheureux does fall in love with the whore – a fact which in itself presents further problems, which can be seen from two standpoints. First, with Freevill we can criticise Malheureux's hypocrisy. When he tells his friend, 'I would but embrace her, hear her speak, and at the most but kiss her' (II. i. 102–3), we can laugh as Marston does at a similar situation described in *The Metamorphosis of Pigmalion's Image*:

> I oft haue smil'd to see the foolery
> Of some sweet Youths, who seriously protest
> That Loue respects not actuall Luxury,
> But onely ioy's to dally, sport and iest:
> Loue is a child, contented with a toy,
> A busk-point, or some fauour still's the boy.[8]

Secondly, however, from Franceschina's standpoint the view becomes more cruel. The prostitute is merely being used without reference to her possible humanity. In order to prevent such a vision, Marston again appeals to humour. Franceschina learning of Freevill's intended marriage is made to look ridiculous. Whilst with her bawd she raves, but on the entrance of Freevill she becomes calm and sweet:

> Franceschina Ick sall be reveng'd! Do ten tousand hell damn me, ick sall have the rogue troat cut; and his love, and his friend, and all his affinity sall smart, sall die, sall hang! Now legion of devil seize him! De

gran' pest, St. Anthony's fire, and de hot Neapolitan poc rot him!

Enter Freevill *and* Malheureux.

Freevill Franceschina!
Franceschina O mine seet, dear'st, kindest, mine loving! O mine tousand, ten tousand, delicated, petty seetart! Ah, mine aderlievest affection!

(*The Dutch Courtesan*, II. ii. 41–9)

Ridicule relieves the possible moral tension, but cannot do so permanently. So as to follow both the Dellio–Cinthye story and the Neo-Platonic concerns and thus expose to Malheureux his inability to distinguish lust from love, Franceschina has to become seriously determined on revenge. Marston therefore has to change again the tone of attitude from ridicule to seriousness as Franceschina is forced by the dictates of plot and theme to utter the truth of her situation:

O unfaithful men – tyrants! betrayers! De very enjoying us loseth us; and, when you only ha' made us hateful, you only hate us. O mine forsaken heart!

(II. ii. 115–18)

Do you take me to be a beast, a creature that for sense only will entertain love, and not only for love, love? O brutish abomination!

(II. ii. 126–8)

The conflicts and inadequacies of the source material become apparent, and we, as an audience, grow perplexed as to how we should react to the whore. Anthony Caputi's response to this problem has been to direct attention to the sub-plot. The 'whole Cocledemoy action,' he tells us, 'serves to adjust the perspective of the Franceschina action by infusing the play with the exuberance of a fabliau.'[9] Others, notably Philip Finkelpearl, have expounded this more fully. Citing William Empson's view that the 'power of suggestion is the strength of the double-plot; once you take the two parts to correspond, any character may take on *mana* because he seems to cause what he corresponds to or be Logos of what he symbolises',[10] Finkelpearl rightly concludes that 'Cocledemoy becomes an antagonist of Malheureux' and Freevill an 'opponent' of Mulligrub.[11] But he ignores the moral problem that the use of the convention naturally proposes in this particular context. In their respective plots Cocledemoy tricks Mulligrub, and Freevill fools Malheureux, but the agents which they use to accomplish their art are vastly different in kind. Whereas Cocledemoy employs inanimate objects – 'the nest of goblets', the 'bag of money', 'the plate', 'the jowl of salmon', 'the cloak' – Freevill's actions employ a human being, Franceschina. By the rule of 'correspondence' in the moral structure of the play, the prostitute is rated no more highly than a bag of gold or a dead fish. The fact that a prostitute is a woman, as capable of human feelings and emotions as anyone else – Freevill, Malheureux or whoever – is tactfully ignored by the philosophy. In contrast, however, the plot demands that she expresses passionate revenge, and we as an audience wonder at the hypocritical cruelty shown to her at the end of the play when she is led off to 'the extremest whip and jail!'[12]

Such is the major critical complaint with the play and one of which Marston himself was aware, since throughout he attempts by various means to disguise the inadequacy. We have already seen how he appeals to both humour and farce as a defence, with only a little success; but his other retreats only intensify the problem. At the centre of these is the character of Freevill.

Until Act IV, scene i, Freevill is portrayed as a man of sense. He follows Montaigne's liberal philosophy and also displays a realisation of the higher values of Platonic love. At first, like Marston's own Pigmalion, Freevill is portrayed as having desired the appearance of beauty. Pigmalion's stone image for him is Franceschina (our complaints once again apply), but he discovers that sensual satisfaction is not enough. Following the Platonic law of ascendancy he casts aside base love for the perfection of Beatrice. Dramatically Marston attempts to accommodate this development through changing the dramatic register from realism to romance. The reality of the gutter and brothel-house are left behind in favour of the poetic convention of the ideal woman. From brothel-house to balcony therefore, Freevill arrives outside Beatrice's chamber:

> The morn is yet but young. Here, gentlemen,
> This is my Beatrice' window, this the chamber
> Of my betrothed dearest, whose chaste eyes,
> Full of lov'd sweetness and clear cheerfulness,
> Have gag'd my soul to her enjoyings,
> Shredding away all those weak under-branches
> Of base affections and unfruitful heats.
> Here bestow your music to my voice.
>
> *Cantat. Exeunt* Gentlemen *with* Pages.
> *Enter* Beatrice *above*.
>
> Always a virtuous name to my chaste love!
>
> (II. i. 1–9)

Such an alteration in the theatrical vehicle is too forced; the demands being made on the audience too great. We cannot believe in the morality of a character who can one moment realistically talk about 'my creature: a pretty, nimble-ey'd Dutch Tanakin . . . a soft, plump, round-cheek'd froe, that has beauty enough for her virtue, virtue enough for a woman' (I. i. 140–3) and the next romantically pledge his life to Beatrice with the words,

> I am sworn all yours.
> No beauty shall untwine our arms, no face
> In my eyes can or shall seem fair;
> And would to God only to me you might
> Seem only fair!
>
> (II. i. 29–33)

Rather we recoil from the situation and tend to see the ironic relevance of Beatrice's own reply:

> Dear, my lov'd heart, be not so passionate;
> Nothing extreme lives long.
>
> (II. i. 49–50)

The problem which we confront, therefore, is that, in attempting to propound a philosophy which in itself is a hybrid of Montaigne and the Neo-Platonists, Marston has been forced to create, in Freevill, a character who is totally inconsistent. Perhaps an answer would be to hold that the dramatist was perfectly aware of what he was doing. If so, Freevill's inconsistency becomes an attempt at a satiric portrait of *amour* conventions such as is found in *The Scourge of Villanie*, where the poetic convention allowed the dramatist the freedom to create a variety of ridiculous lovers, Martius, Publius, Saturio and so forth, within the compass of a few lines.[13] Dramatic convention, however, can accommodate such satirical juxtapositioning within a single character only if it has been made clear from the beginning that the convention is satiric, satiric–romantic or moral, but not naturalistic. Such a statement cannot be given by Marston, since the Montaigne philosophy which he is following throughout requires a solid – and unattractive – realism, where the Neo-Platonism demands a certain abstraction. There is no answer. The audience can only be perplexed by the conflicting interests, and we can only reject Freevill's excuses and with them the philosophies implied:

> I lov'd her [Franceschina] with my heart until my soul showed me the imperfection of my body, and placed my affection on a lawful love, my modest Beatrice. . . .
>
> (I. ii. 89–92)

Throughout the drama Marston attempts further defences of this major weakness, but in doing so he often exacerbates rather than solves the problem. A case in point, as John O'Connor has pointed out,[14] is the inconsistencies exposed by Freevill's speech at IV. ii. 31–47, in which the rake suddenly becomes the moral teacher of 'repentance'. Malheureux is to be condemned and so brought to his senses for the very sin Freevill has committed and advocated:

> Now repentance, the fool's whip, seize thee!
> Nay, if there be no means I'll be thy friend.
> But not thy vice's; and with greatest sense
> I'll force thee feel thy errors to the worst.
>
> (IV. ii. 31–4)

If within the dramatic convention of the work we had witnessed a credible development in Freevill's own character from lascivious youth to respectable husband, such a moral aim would seem justified. As it is, it appears hypocritical and again only illustrates the irrelevance of the dramatic theme in the context of the play's mixed conventions. By Act IV, any connection between Freevill and Montaigne's and Castiglione's philosophies has long since disappeared from the audience's attention, and thus his speech is seen merely as a crude device to ensure a smoother conclusion to the plot.

A more successful defence employed is the creation of an alternative moral teacher, Crispinella. Of all the characters in the play she is the most credible, since she never suffers from being transferred from one dramatic convention to another. Instead she becomes a mouthpiece for some of Montaigne's more acceptable sentiments. Thus even in her own inconsistency (like Shakespeare's Beatrice in *Much Ado About Nothing*, she will never marry but eventually does so) Crispinella illustrates a warm honesty of character. She advocates truth rather than hypocrisy, realism rather than romance, and virtue rather than moral pretension:

> For my own part, I consider nature without apparel; without disguising of custom or compliment, I give thoughts words, and words truth, and truth boldness. She whose honest freeness makes it her virtue to speak what she thinks will make it her necessity to think what is good.
>
> (III. i. 34–9)

Fittingly, therefore, it is she who rebukes Freevill (V. ii. 58) for his treatment of Beatrice in feigning his death. But, quite revealingly, it is she also whom Marston never allows to be involved with the Franceschina story. Crispinella remains silent during the action of anagnorisis (v. iii), for if Marston had put words in her mouth her character would have demanded the right to criticise the whole unstable fabric of the plot's mixed conventions and dubious philosophy. She would have had to take up the cause of the wronged Franceschina.

Despite all these reservations about *The Dutch Courtesan*, the play cannot be dismissed as irrelevant. In it Marston shows himself as a dramatist grappling with the technical problems of construction which at about the same time were troubling Shakespeare. The difficulties with the play are not unlike those encountered in *Much Ado About Nothing*, *All's Well That Ends Well* and *Measure For Measure*, in which the thematic concerns impinge upon dramatic structure and credibility and theatrical convention on moral philosophy. It is a problem which Marston never did conquer and which Shakespeare solved perhaps only in *The Tempest*.

We encounter similar problems when we consider another drama over which Marston at least had some influence, *The Insatiate Countess*. The authorship problem of this play has in the past caused many to forget that we have a drama in existence which was performed at the Whitefriars and which still deserves our attention, even though we are waiting for a textual study to distinguish the varying hands that worked at its composition.[15]

The aim of *The Insatiate Countess* is the antithesis of that found in *Sophonisba*. Instead of the glory of the female sex we are to witness its shame and dishonour. To illustrate this, however, it was possible to employ a similar structure to that found in *Sophonisba*, and thus within *The Insatiate Countess* there is evidence of an attempt to balance characters in the tradition of a morality play. On the side of good there is Roberto; on that of evil, Isabella; and between, as a composite *Humanum Genus*, Massino, Gniaca and Don Sago. With the agent of good there is a successful attempt at stylisation rather than characterisation. Roberto appears as a symbol and consequently illustrates little emotion on discovering Isabella's infidelity:

> Since I cannot
> Enjoy the noble title of a man,
> But after-ages, as our vertues are
> Buryed whilst we are living, will sound out
> My infamie, and her degenerate shame;
> Yet in my life ile somther't if I may,
> And, like a dead man, to the world bequeath
> These houses of vanitie, Mils and Lands.
> Take what you will, I will not keepe among you Servants,
> And welcome some religious Monasterie,

A true sworne Beads-man Ile hereafter be,
And wake the morning cocke with holy prayers.
(*The Insatiate Countess*, p. 35)[16]

With Christian Stoicism, therefore, he condemns her sin but recoils from exposing her 'shame', and thus takes refuge in the monastery. Similarly, at the end of the play he is portrayed as the good man stunned by his wife's folly in comparison with his true virtue:

For he [that] once lov'd her, lends his pined corps,
Motion to bring him to her stage of honour
Where drown'd in woe at her so dismall chance,
He claspes her: thus. [*He fals into a trance.*]
(p. 73)

Such heavy symbolism serves well enough but is not counterweighted in kind by the other figures in the morality structure. Isabella in particular should be illustrated in terms of evil alone, but in her portrayal the authors become involved in morality problems not unlike those experienced with the Freevill–Franceschina relationship. From the start of the play Isabella is illustrated as desiring sexual freedom. Her first speech raises questions concerning her relationship with her former husband. He apparently in his jealousy kept her under lock and key, but, as the plot begins to illustrate, he may well have had just cause for his action. In speaking of his conduct Isabella wishes him buried 'tenne cubites deeper', to make sure he will not rise again, but she continues by advocating liberality for her sex:

I am free as ayre. You of my sexe,
In the first flow of youth use you the sweets
Due to your proper beauties, ere the ebbe
And long waine of unwelcome change shall come.
Faire women play: she's chaste whom none will have.
(p. 6)

The idea that women should not waste their youth is familiar in the Renaissance,[17] but spoken by a lady in mourning it (along with her other sentiments) comes as a surprise and consequently as a testimony to her wantonness. It begins a slight but significant form of characterisation which in itself would not detract from the morality structure if it were not for the way in which her relationship with Massino is described. In tempting him Isabella shows hesitancy about her conduct. She worries about her social standing and her reputation. Thus, in quizzing the page who is to deliver her love-letter, she displays human concern:

Isabella Tell me true,
Dost thou not thinke the Letter is of Love?
Page If you would have me thinke so Madame, yes.
Isabella What dost thou thinke thy Lady is so fond?
Give me the Letter, thy selfe shall see it.
Yet I should teare it in the breaking ope,
And make him lay a wrongfull charge on thee,
. . .
But 'tis all one, the Letter is not of Love. . . .
(pp. 30–1)

To compensate for such worries in the vice figure, Massino therefore has to be portrayed as encouraging the adultery rather than merely falling for the woman's charms:

Ile teach you how to woo.
Say you have lov'd me long,
And tell me that a woman's feeble tongue
Was never tuned unto a wooing-string;
Yet for my sake you will forget your sexe,
And court my Love with strain'd Immodestie,
Then bid me make you happy with a kisse.
(p. 32)

There is therefore an immediate conflict between the overall structure of the play and the role of the characters. Whereas the morality form demands symbolic characters, Isabella is given at least a social conscience and Massino is promiscuous enough to encourage her into evil. The problem is exacerbated later in the action when, like Freevill, Massino suddenly transforms into a figure of morality, rebuking his friend Gniaca for becoming 'onely flesh without a soule' (p. 57). The conversion, however, has not been caused, as in Freevill's case, by a sudden revelation of Platonic beauty, but rather by Isabella's rejection of Massino. His virtue is built first on the foundation of hurt pride and later on the interests of self-protection, since in railing at the countess he has endangered his own life. The morality structure of the play cannot accommodate the inconsistencies of either of these characters, the male-biased philosophy implicit in Medina's judgement of Don Sago and Isabella. Whereas the countess is condemned to death for finally instigating the death of Massino, the actual murderer, her new lover, Don Sago, is forgiven his crime and promoted in the army (p. 69). The whole business lacks even the semblance of honesty.

There are, however, some redeeming features. The sub-plot attempts to compensate for the male bias in the main plot, since it is the husbands Rogero and Claridiana who become the butt of the satire. They are ridiculed not only for their hatred of one another but also for attempting to use their wives as weapons in their private battle. Rogero tries to humiliate Claridiana by sleeping with his wife, and Claridiana to cuckold Rogero by sleeping with his wife. The respective wives prove too clever for their husbands and so also exchange beds. The men sleep with their own wives and their imaginations, as the ladies later discuss, prove to be a strong aphrodisiac:

Abigail O wench, imagination is strong in pleasure.
Thais That's true: for the opinion my Good-man had of enjoying you, made him doe wonders.
Abigail Why shold weake man, that is so soon satisfied, desire variety?
Thais Their answere is, to feed on Phesants continually would breede a loathing.
Abigail Then if we seeke for strange flesh that have stomackes at will, 'tis pardonable.
Thais I, if men had any feeling of it, but they judge us by themselves.

(p. 45)

Similar comedy is found throughout the main and the sub-plots. In the former, however, it merely adds to the confusion of the variety of conventions being employed by the dramatists. Thus, although Don Sago is reminiscent of Don Quixote or the later Knight of the Burning Pestle, his comic portraiture becomes inconsistent with his serious mission to kill Massino. In the sub-plot, fortunately, the satire is virtually free from similar hindrances. Mendoza is caricatured as a traditional lover farcically attempting to enter Lentulus's house via her bedroom's balcony. Charging the gods to punish him if he intends to stain his lady's 'Honor with foule lust' (p. 37) he climbs the ladder. Presumably hearing his request, the gods grant it, and poor Mendoza falls from the top rung. A traditional romance attitude, as epitomised in *Romeo and Juliet*'s balcony scene, is the successful target of the dramatist's humour.

The Mendoza story in the sub-plot is never completed in the play and thereby perhaps shows the difficulties which the authors themselves found in attempting to integrate so many differing modes and themes into a single drama. It is not unfair to say that the play contains examples of the majority of early themes, mistakes and experiments which Marston tried to conquer in his major works. It is for this reason that we perhaps have the impression that Marston's hand in the play is of an earlier rather than a later date.[18] Whichever, in its embryonic form *The Insatiate Countess* is valuable as a contrast with the plays in which Marston was able to develop his experiments to a more satisfactory conclusion.

5
Entertainment and Artistry

It often seems more than difficult to assess the tenor of Marston's plays and this is particularly true of the lesser-known works. The text, as stated earlier, is only a component of the 'play', and despite all the vast scholarship the intentions behind the original production necessarily appear cloudy and ill defined. Too frequently when arguing the case for the satiric nature of a drama, in the context particularly of the war of the theatres, we find ourselves in the end confessing that we can prove little. We are working on instinct, intuition and hypothesis, and, although fragments of evidence reinforce our speculation, in conclusion we can only suggest. This is particularly true of plays such as *The Insatiate Countess* or *Jack Drum's Entertainment*. M. C. Andrews, for example, has seen certain evidence of a satiric relationship between the latter and a 'roughly contemporaneous' play, *The Trial of Chivalry*; but, since we do not know which of these plays was performed first, Mr Andrews can in the end only speculate that *Jack Drum* was written after *The Trial* and that Marston knew the earlier work: 'That *The Trial* is the earlier play seems certain. Marston could have converted romance into burlesque (as he does with *Arcadia*); it appears highly unlikely that the author of *The Trial* reversed the process, and converted burlesque into romance.'[1]

This is common-sense, but it is only a speculative point which might retain weight if companion arguments tended to substantiate it. This they do not. It is merely the tone of *Jack Drum* that leads to further conjecture. Few if any verbal parallels are found between the two plays and we gain the impression that evidence for an independent use of *The Arcadia* by both dramatists is the only true discovery to be made. When we are told,

> there is an important indication that Marston was familiar with both versions [*The Arcadia* and *The Trial of Chivalry*]. The scene in which Katherine, thinking Pasquil dead, prepares to stab herself, seems based upon the similar scene involving the Katharine of *The Trial of Chivalry*: despite important differences, each presents the abortive suicide of a lady who believes that she is sacrificing herself where her beloved died, but who is interrupted by the lover before she can perform the heroic but unwarranted action[2]

we must wonder whether the 'important differences' are due to the fact that both dramatists are conducting a variation on a romance theme epitomised in *Romeo and Juliet*, a play at a height of popularity around the time that both *The Trial* and *Jack Drum* were written. This may or may not be so and we are not refuting Mr Andrews's hypothesis but merely showing how speculative such criticism necessarily has to be.

Ironically, where Foakes has perhaps been a slight disservice to minor dramatists is in his perceptive essay on *The Comedy of Errors*,[3] where he has been able to show that the Shakespearean play goes beyond the realms of mere entertainment and escapism towards something of a deeper literary significance. It is, however, unfortunate that in following this depth of criticism when dealing with dramatists such as Marston, other critics have concluded that because some plays are no more than entertainments they may be dismissed as irrelevant. This of course is where Richard Levin's approach is dangerous.[4] *Jack Drum's Entertainment* is a case in point. The work is not great literature or literature at all. It does not profess to be so, but it does seem to be the ground plan of a successful theatrical event. It claims only to be an entertainment, nothing more nor less, and it is on this definition that we should judge it.

Anthony Caputi has already seen a resemblance between the entertainment and those of the *commedia dell 'arte*,[5] and certainly we can imagine that if the play were to be produced today it would easily lend itself to a Clifford Williams form of *commedia* production.[6] It employs a number of stock characters in a series of comic episodes revolving around three ingredients: love, the fool and money. Most of the episodes balance themselves with another, as do the characters, all of which are exaggeratedly drawn and presented in a pantomime tableau usually separated by a song, a dance or a grotesque interlude. The very introduction sets the atmosphere, with one of the tiremen entering to complain of his treatment by the author backstage. There is obviously noise and confusion coming from the tiring-house, and this tireman is some sort of clown thrown onto the stage for a prologue. With comic amateurishness his introduction is briefly given and he exits. We imagine more noise backstage, as presumably he is told that he is no more than an idiot, before 'one of the children' enters to 'improvise' amends by promising a play in which the author,

> vowes not to torment your listning eares
> With mouldy fopperies of stale Poetry,
> Unpossible drie mustie Fictions.
>
> (*Jack Drum's Entertainment*, p. 179)[7]

This is not to be a pretentious, literary performance but a comic entertainment. Jack Drum and Timothy Twedle then introduce themselves and the performance with a few bawdy jokes, and straightaway Twedle gives the audience a tune on his pipe. It is a firm, well-thought-out comic introduction. As the tune comes to its end the first real caricatures enter. Sir Edward Fortune, plainly a simple but honest knight philosophising in his drink, accompanied by M. Mamon, bespectacled and supporting a huge comic nose. No sooner have they introduced themselves than a morris troupe enters for a song and a dance. The tone of the occasion has adequately been set and is to continue in this vein. The work contains at least a dozen songs or dances in its course, together with many comic, grotesque and melodramatic devices which we now associate with pantomime and other traditional forms of festive entertainment.

One such grotesque tableau comes with the presentation of a satirical rogues gallery towards the end of Act I. It is introduced by the appearance of two pages giving a small but curious interlude not immediately related to anything that has preceded their entrance but serving as a brief commentary on the whole concept of the work:

Enter two Pages, the one laughing, the other crying.

Page 1 Why do'st thou crie?
Page 2 Why do'st thou laugh?
Page 1 I laugh to see thee crie.
Page 2 And I crie to see thee laugh.
Peace be to us. Heres our Maisters.
(p. 191)

This is a ridiculous – almost absurd – picture, but it tells us what is happening as on one hand the melodrama and on the other the rather trite humour are produced. It is a traditional pantomime technique, used for example by Clifford Williams, the lesser *commedia* figures giving a brief tableau of the emotions and reactions that are occurring both on the stage and in the audience. The scene that follows is designed to have us in tears with either laughter or 'despair' as Brabant Senior displays the caricatures Puffe, Ellis, and Mounsieur John fo de King. The figures portray their humours and perhaps are as Finkelpearl postulates, satirical portraits of people readily known to the audience.[8] This again can only be a matter of speculation, but, if they were, the comic effect would only have been increased.

The picture-gallery presentation of this 'feast of fools' is complemented in the second act, after another song of course, by the obviously favourite comic balcony scenes.[9] Marston at the beginning of this act presents three balcony episodes in rapid succession, two comic, one melodramatic. The damsel on each occasion is Katherine. The affected pipe-smoking Puffe begins the sequence but runs out of natural puff, only to be rejected:

> Page Nay if he be puffing once, the fire of his wit is out.
> Puffe Why she is gone. Hart did I rise for this?
> Page She cannot endure puffing. O you puft her away.
> Puffe Lets slink along unseen, 'tis yet scarse day.
>
> (p. 196)

It is plain that he is not just annoyed that his heart rose for love, but that he did from his bed at such an inordinate hour. It is now the turn of big-nosed Mamon, guaranteed to produce a laugh before he speaks, who, preceded by his clown Flawne 'bearing a light', enters stealthily. They move around the stage for a little time, conducting some traditional comic business before Flawne, reflecting on the comedy they are producing, talks to the audience.

> Flawne Now me thinks I hold the candle to the divel.
> Mamon Put out the light, the day begins to breake.
> Flawne Would the day and thy neck were broke togither.
>
> (p. 196)

There is a short implicit pause at this point as Mamon humorously surveys the situation before setting in motion the next routine for comic interchange, produced by him hobbling:

> Mamon Oh how the gout and love do tyre me.
> Flawne Why sir, love is nothing but the very gout.
> Mamon As how *Flawne*? as how?
> Flawne Thus sir: Gout and love, both come with Idlenesse, both incurable, both humourous, onely this difference: the Gout causeth a great tumour in a mans legges, and love a great swelling in a womans belly.
> Mamon Why then ô Love, ô Gout, ô goutie Love, how thou torments olde *Mamon*. . . .
>
> (pp. 196–7)

Katherine again appears at the balcony, which gives a cue for a ridiculous song from Flawne. This Mamon introduces with 'List to the Musicke that corrupts the Goddes, / Subverts even Desteny, and thus it shogges' (p. 197). It fails, however, to corrupt this Goddess, and Mamon is dismissed for the entrance of the true lover, Pasquill. Here Marston neatly changes the tenor from farce to melodrama as Mamon scuttles off into the shadows to witness Pasquill's successful avowal of love.

The ensuing dialogue between the true lovers is deliberately balanced between playful comedy and sentimentalism, drawing the traditional pantomime response from the audience but with the added impetus of Mamon for the most part lurking in the shade. The love scene completed, the large-nosed caricature reappears, now firmly as the villain of the piece. We can imagine him with Pantalone's cloak or a nineteenth-century villain's cape as with John fo de King he lays his evil plots. From here on Mamon serves as the catalyst for the action that is to ensue, action which through its melodrama is to satirise the whole romantic conception of the lover. Katherine and Pasquill's antics, whether based on characters in *The Arcadia*, *The Trial of Chivalry* or *Romeo and Juliet*, serve generally as a satiric portrait of the lover, a character who can be naturally absurd to all but his partner. Thus, on thinking that Pasquill has been killed – like Antonio, Pasquill fails to tell his love of his feigned death – Katherine exaggeratedly contemplates suicide without even trying first to discover if the rumour is true:

> Now thou immortall spirit of my Love,
> Thou pretious soule of *Pasquil* view this knife
> Which once thou gavest me, and prepare thy arme
> To clip the spirit of thy constant Love.
> Dear *Ned* I come, by death I will be thine,
> Since life denies it to poore *Katherine*.
>
> (p. 214–15)

The knife, of course, was originally given to her by the 'dead' Pasquill, a fact which raises the melodrama and sentimentalism. Pasquill with similar melodramatic inevitability appears at this critical moment to rescue his love from death's clutches:

> Hold, hold, thou miracle of constancie,
> First let heaven perish, and the crazde world runne
> Into first *Chaos* of confusion,
> Before such cruell violence be done
> To her faire breast, whose fame by vertue wonne,
> Shall honour women whilst there shines a sunne.
>
> (p. 215)

The dramatic tenor of the whole entertainment shows how this scene is to be regarded: not as serious drama but as pantomime burlesque. But all is not over. Rescued once, the damsel, clad only in a petticoat (p. 214), to emphasise her vulnerability, again falls foul of the wicked Mamon's malice, that 'venombd foame, / That poisoned all the sweets of our content' (p. 216). Captured by the villain, Katherine has a vile liquid poured over her face so as to disfigure her.

Mamon I, I will rest, and thou shalt rest thus blur'd,
Thus poysond; venomde with the oyle of Toades:
If *Mamon* cannot get thee, none shall joy
Which he could not enjoy. I feare no lawe,
Gold in the firmest conscience makes a flawe.
Rot like to *Helen*: *Spittle* hence, adiew,
Let *Pasquil* boast in your next interview.

(p. 217)

We almost expect to hear this speech end with a nineteenth-century 'Ha! ha!' and the wicked grin as the empty bottle has been thrust away, the sadistic quip given and the heroine left in utter despair. Katherine rushes off to hide in disgrace, whilst Pasquill in dismay loses his sanity (pp. 225, 235), until a skilful 'Bedlame' (p. 235) miraculously restores Katherine to health.

The main plot, therefore, is an exaggerated story with villains, magicians and lovers which as it progresses is balanced by humour and farce both within its development, as for example when Pasquill rises from the 'dead' to beat Mamon over the head in Punch and Judy fashion (p. 202), and in the contrasting sub-plots. These give an excuse for an intensification of the comedy and the satiric themes. Jack Drum's and Mounsieur's rivalry over Winifred, which concludes in the sack routine, is a typical piece of Tudor farce, reminiscent of *Gammer Gurton's Needle*, and only tenuously related to the Katherine–Pasquill situation. The Brabant–Camelia sub-plot, however, has closer associations, which further the general satiric purpose. The situation here is the reverse of the main plot, with the true lover Brabant being rejected at his love's window (p. 203) and having to suffer by seeing the fool Ellis subsequently rewarded (p. 204). The story leads to another attempted murder and suicide (pp. 231–2), but the hero in this case is presented sympathetically, as a character who commits crimes similar to Mamon's but, as the audience realise, does so owing to his understandable distraction rather than avaricious villainy. In terms of a general satiric picture being drawn, we might postulate that if there is anything of real literary or moral significance in the play it might be found within this comparison of Brabant's and Mamon's attitudes, in that Mamon is plainly an embodiment of what L. C. Knights has referred to as the 'anti-acquisitive' attitude prevailing in much of the city comedy of the time. [10] It would be wrong, however, to overstress this example, as it would to emphasise that the character of Sir Edward Fortune might be seen in the debate concerning not only the wise employment of finance but also the parents' control over their children's future. Such themes are to be expected in any comic satire or entertainment of the time, much as we readily expect and accept in many of our present-day comic shows a satiric jest at South African policies or Britain's economic crisis. It is merely a matter of employing contemporary issues to aid the popular appeal of the entertainment. It is something which Marston proves that he can handle quite adequately in what was plainly a very funny entertainment.

As more an entertainment than a serious play, *What You Will* is, in its design, similar in aim and quality to *Jack Drum*. As with the earlier work, *What You Will* gives the impression of being in practice a light and episodic but nevertheless comic piece. If we look at the play's narrative progression, many scenes, such as the schoolmaster and mock-trial episodes, appear to be redundant and irrelevant, and characters often seem to appear on stage for no particular reason. Quadratus, Lampatho and Simplicius, for example, arrive at Laverdure's room at the beginning of Act II without our being aware that they were planning to meet him. Celia, around whom the whole narrative revolves, does not make an appearance until Act IV, scene i, and as with *Jack Drum* any linear development is continually halted by songs and dances. Yet, as we found with the former entertainment, the Induction instructs us that we should not expect a play in the accepted sense:

Atticus	. . . lets see what stuffe must cloath our eares what's the plaies name?
Phylomuse	*What You Will.*
Doricus	*Ist Comedy, Tragedy, Pastorall, Morall, Nocturnal*, or *Historie?*
Phylomuse	Faith perfectly neither, but even *What You Will*, a slight toye, lightly composed, to swiftly finisht, ill plotted, worse written, I feare me worst acted, and indeed *What You Will*.

(*What You Will*, p. 233)[11]

There is an obvious dose of comic modesty here, but nevertheless the atmosphere is being set. Before speaking, Atticus, Doricus and Phylomuse have been sitting 'a good while' (p. 231) on the stage and their first words have been directed at someone sitting close to them in the auditorium:

Doricus O Fie some lights, sirs fie, let there be no deeds of darknesse done among us – I so, so, pree thee Tyerman set *Sineor Snuffe* a fier, he's a chollerick Gentleman, he will take Pepper in the nose instantly, feare not, fore Heaven I wonder they tollerate him so nere the Stage. (p. 231)

The audience is being brought into the conduct and humour of the piece right from the start. With them, as in *Jack Drum*, the dramatist himself is also drawn into the comic repartee: 'Shall he be creastfalne if some looser braine, / In flux of witte uncively befilth / His slight composures?' (pp. 231–2). The induction is designed to create the comic milieu of the work. This is not a traditional play but a 'what you will', an entertainment or perhaps what might in modern terminology be called a revue, with comedy, satire and song. As such it is rather interesting, since it is within a tradition still in vogue in the twentieth-century England of the university satirists: the revue-type humour of men such as Peter Cooke, Dudley Moore, John Wells, John Fortune and Jonathan Miller.[12] In the same way as these have over the past twenty years chosen the episodic form to convey their satiric vision, so the seventeenth-century Middle Temple wit, Marston, employs a similar medium. Thus within a loose narrative framework Marston is able to interpolate scenes of ludicrous fun and cynicism in a manner which today we expect from such a figure as John Cleese.

In an attempt to discover the true satiric nature of *What You Will*, critics, especially those involved in the war-of-the-theatres debate, have tended to lose sight of this obvious humour, and consequently it has often been seen as a tedious contribution to an esoteric argument. To some extent Finkelpearl has attempted to redress the balance with his insistence that the 'tone is one of boisterous gaiety in the tradition of "festive comedy"'.[13] Certainly within the drama we find the loss-of-identity motif, which can be taken within the context of a serious thematic concern, as can the satiric natures of Lampatho and Quadratus. But, whilst all this is there, the main concern of the play is the entertainment it provides and the way in which it does it. If, for example, as Finkelpearl postulates, the character of Lampatho is more in keeping with a satiric portrait of Marston himself than with one of Ben Jonson – which is an interesting suggestion, although again one hard to prove – then the *tour de force* of this situation in comic terms is almost inestimable.[14] Here we may have a writer, subject to the wrath of Jonson, mimicking some of his traits rather than those of his adversary on stage: a John Cleese laughing at some of John Cleese's characteristics. If so it would shed a new light on the conduct of the war-of-the-theatres; but at this distance, as Finkelpearl intimates, little more can be said.[15]

More, however, can be discussed about the way in which Marston does create the comic effect within the play. To a large extent this revolves around the complex and what has been called confused characterisation of Quadratus.[16] He is without doubt a difficult figure to set in a critical box, whether it be labelled Epicurean, Stoic or satirist. In the practicalities of his stage behaviour the 'fat and therefore faithfull' (p. 290) character seems to have a certain relationship to the Falstaff of *Henry IV*[17] in his desire to be the centre of comic attention. This means that, like Falstaff, Quadratus is perfectly able to change his whole attitude to a certain situation or development in order to remain a lord of misrule. The man who counts with Quadratus is Quadratus. He can be an Epicurean Stoic as easily as Falstaff can be a cowardly hero. This ability of variance in a role so as to keep command is something which Hal easily sees and plays upon with Falstaff and which, therefore, through the prince as commentator and manipulator, is made clear to the audience. In Marston's entertainment, however, there is no such linking character between the stage and audience; no serious world of politics through which the antics of misrule can be judged. The state of Venice is as misruled and comically caricatured as Quadratus, Laverdure or Lampatho themselves. Thus at the end of the play there is no tragic rejection of the king of humour, but rather a mere yet annoying postponement of his *Cato Utican* scene:

Quadratus And Ile curse you all.
O yee ha interrupt a sceane.
Duke *Quadratus* we will heare these pointes discussed,
With apter and more calme affected houres.
Quadratus Well, good, good.
(p. 294)

Quadratus is only slightly deflated because he has lost the centre of attention. He is soon back in the limelight humorously suggesting to the despairing Lampatho,

Why marry me.
Thou canst have but soft flesh, good bloud, sound bones.
And that which fils up all your bracks, good stones
(p. 294)

and bringing the play to a close with the prospect of Rhenish wine.

This ability at adaptation and desire for comic superiority is the essence of Quadratus and is seen particularly vividly in Act II, scene i, in which his role as master is challenged. The comic artistry of this scene is quite complex. Very early in the play we have been encouraged by the author to regard Quadratus, through his 'Hate all things' speech to Iacomo, as the scathing cynic. Act II, scene i, opens by presenting a perfect victim for the cynic's humour. Laverdure is a man in love with appearance, and therefore well created for the general appearance-and-reality theme of the entertainment as a whole. Thus the first appearance of the caricature, 'sitting on his bed apparalling himselfe', affected in speech, thought and manner, gently sets the comic tone. Quadratus and his friends enter and immediately Quadratus cracks a one-off joke: *Phœbus, Phœbe*, Sunne, Moone, and seaven Starres make thee the dilling of Fortune, my sweet *Laverdure*, my rich *French* bloud, ha yee deere rogue, hast any pudding *Tobacco*?' From the first line of the joke we do not know what to expect. The 'pudding *Tobacco*' request comes as the absurd kick in the tail. It is simply a joke maintaining, perhaps slightly increasing, the gentle humour. It is at this point, however, that the complex comedy of the scene begins, since Simplicius and Lampatho take over the role of *agents provocateurs* of humour against Laverdure. In so doing they immediately endanger the comic authority of Quadratus. Sensing the challenge and the slim possibility of his usurpation from being comic master, Quadratus therefore changes his attack. Laverdure becomes insignificant as a victim; rather it is Quadratus's friends who are to bear his charge,

> Is not this rare now: now by *Gorgons* head,
> I gape and am struck stiffe in wonderment,
> At sight of these strange beasts. Yon *Chamblet* youth,
> *Symplicius Faber* that *Hermaphrodite*
> *Party par pale*, that bastard Moungerell soule,
> Is nought but admiration and applause,
> Of yon *Lampatho Doria*, a fustie caske,
> Devote to mouldy customes of hoary eld.
>
> (p. 246)

Quadratus has made himself an outsider to the proposed main line of comedy and become the commentator in direct contact with the audience. He turns and points out the humour in the jokesters, thus re-establishing himself with the audience as chief comedian. Added as an essential ingredient to this is the fact that his satire of Lampatho involves the audience's knowledge of the war-of-the-theatres, although, as we have seen, since Finkelpearl's book, we may not be able to identify fully the exact character of the literary satiric attack. It is not enough, however, for Quadratus merely to convince the audience of his superiority. As a character in the play he has still to prove his mastery to Lampatho and Simplicius, who have unwittingly challenged it. Herein can lie some of our troubles in knowing how to approach the man. For, in re-establishing his position amongst his fictitious companions, Quadratus has to relinquish his new-formed intellectual relationship with the audience as commentator and so again becomes an absurd figure whom the audience laughs *at* rather than *with*. He immediately goes into battle on Laverdure's side:

> I protest beleeve him not, Ile beg thee *Laverdure*
> For a conceal'd Ideot if thou credit him,
> Hee's a *Hyena*, and with *Civitt* scent
> Of perfum'd words, drawes to make a prey
> For laughter of thy credit.
>
> (p. 247)

Lampatho, who does not realise that the battle has begun, continues to lead his satiric attack on Laverdure and calls on Quadratus for extra ammunition and reinforcements: 'O *Pallas! Quadratus*, harke, harke, a most compleat phantasma, a most ridiculous humor, preethee shoot him through and through with a jest, make him lye by the lee, thou *Basilisco* of witte' (p. 247). This is all that Quadratus needs. With a charge on Lampatho he re-establishes himself as a lord,

> *Gnathonicall* Coxcombe!
>
> Why thou *Pole-head*, thou *Ianus*, thou *poultron*, thou protest, thou Eare-wig that wrigglest into mens braines: thou durty cur that be-mierst with thy fawning, thou –
>
> (p. 248)

Poor Lampatho is completely set back by the onslaught. If anyone is a Janus, Quadratus is the man, but Lampatho has no time to object as the fat man raves into comic absurdities:

> Ha, he! mount *Chirall* on the wings of fame!
> A horse, a horse, my kingdom for a horse!
> Looke the, I speake play scrappes. *Bydet* Ile downe:
> Sing, sing, or stay – weele quaffe or any thing:
> *Rivo, Saint Marke*, lets talke as loose as ayre,
> Un-wind youthes coullors, display our selves
> So that yon envy-starved Curre may yealpe
> And spend his chappes at our Phantasticknesse.
>
> (p. 248)

The gentle laughter that began the scene has accelerated towards uncontrolled hilarity. By referring to *Don Kynsayder* Quadratus attempts to keep a grip on his wit and, more importantly, the consequent rapport with his audience. But it is of little avail, since the audience will now be laughing at him in his bombast absurdity. Furiously he continues to bear down on his victim (p. 249), although at the right moment there comes an alteration in the pace of the scene, and therefore a break of relief for the audience as Laverdure intervenes for the first time as peace-maker: 'Tut *Via* let all runne and glib and square' (p. 249). Quadratus, as lord of misrule, has admirably broken the intended course of the comedy so to increase the comic effect. No one on stage really knows where the comedy is to lead, but certainly Quadratus is the master of it. He continually changes his tone and his pace as he goes along. He does not weaken his attack on Lampatho, but now independent he is also able to take a satiric attitude towards Laverdure, until finally he runs out of breath:

Laverdure Hast not runne thy selfe out of breath, bulley?
Quadratus And I have not jaded thy eares more then I have tierd my tongue, I could runne discourse, put him out of his full pace.
  I could poer speech till thou crid'st ho, but troth, I dread a glut. . . .

(p. 251)

At the end of this speech there would probably be a slight pause for actors and audience to regain their breath and composure before Laverdure, peace-maker still, restarts: 'Come all merth and solace, capers, healthes and whiffes!' (p. 251). Quadratus, having proved his comic authority, consents, and Lampatho, in submission – '& ther's my hand; I imbrace you, love you, nay adore thee, for by the juice of worm-woode, thou has a bitter braine' (p. 251) – also agrees. This masterful comic scene comes to an end with dancing and songs. Only tenuously related to the play's narrative, though certainly attached to its themes, the episode stands out as one in a number of scenes designed for their intrinsic entertainment value in performance. As soon as Lampatho, Quadratus, Simplicius and Laverdure have left the stage at the conclusion of the episode, a new scene, but one with a similar festive character, begins, a burlesque comedy about a school lesson. Marston's artistry in entertainment is apparent in this clever variation of a 'what you will' theme. The situation of schoolboys mocking their masters by impersonating a grammar lesson is perfectly appropriate for a feast-of-fools revelry, if indeed this play, like its Shakespearean namesake, *Twelfth Night* or *What You Will*, was performed for Twelfth Night.[18] Marston's artistry, however, is not merely in varying his theme, thus retaining the comic atmosphere without the danger of monotony, but also in the way that once he has established his new direction he shows the ability to recount his former variation. As soon as the schoolboy comedy has been established and the Quadratus episode begins to fade into the background, the fat comic is suddenly reintroduced. We immediately react to the humour that he symbolises, and thus the two comic themes join in a total revelry as Quadratus pleads mercy for Holifernes. In this manner the figure of Quadratus provides the play with a unity throughout. He, as critic, commentator, satirist, humorist, is the main element of the entertainment. The comedy, the songs and the dances rely on a statement which he essentially embodies and certainly symbolises. Thus, once he has joined the schoolboy farce, a further impetus is given to the entertainment and this results in a further song. Moreover, since Lampatho and Simplicius have entered with him, an excuse is given for the start of the next satiric episode, which is to accommodate Lampatho's renowned 'spaniel' speech followed by more railing from the satiric commentator. The unifying element of *What You Will*, therefore, despite the Celia story, seems not to be the linear narrative so much as the embodiment of humour in the satiric clown and lord, Quadratus.

Although immensely funny in his comic role, Quadratus, as also Marston's critic–commentator in *What You Will*, still finds some of his ancestry in Feliche and Pandulpho and anticipates some of the traits of Malevole and the *The Fawn*'s Duke Hercules. The different approach to all these characters, however, is marked. Quadratus's function is to rail, and his inconsistency in choosing his targets is deliberately wayward so as to increase the comedy. Feliche, Pandulpho and Malevole, as we have seen, also show inconsistencies, but their waywardness to a large extent depends on plot developments in a manner that Quadratus's do not. Within this tradition of the critic, however, Duke Hercules differs from them all in that he is probably the least wayward of them. Although he is ready to adapt to new situations, we feel right from the beginning of the play that he is in total command of the overall position. Unlike Quadratus he does not have to fight for authority as lord of misrule, and unlike Malevole he has not had his political authority usurped, but, rather, has freely and only temporarily relinquished it. Thus, as Joel Kaplan in his fine article on the play has said, 'We are most likely to refer to "Malevole" as the central character of *The Malcontent*, but think of Hercules, not "Faunus", as the dominant figure in *The Fawn*.'[19] Both dukes assume a disguise, but, whereas in *The Malcontent* the role being played is shown first, and the actor, only vaguely, later, in *The Fawn* it is the duke who first appears and he takes on his disguise in full view of the audience. We are, of course, back to a favourite Marston technique: that of presenting characters as actors. But, whether the act or the character is presented first, the moral problems which we encountered in the *Antonio* plays and *The Malcontent* again deserve our attention with *The Fawn*.

The man who at the beginning of *The Fawn* is to assume a new role is a duke. To play the spy on his son Tiberio, Hercules, like Vincentio of Shakespeare's *Measure for Measure*, relinquishes his responsibilities of state. At first it could appear that audience reaction to the situation might agree with Renaldo's apprehension at such a deed. A moral question seems to be involved here, as it is with Vincentio. Is Hercules going to be the foolish man who assumes that he can abdicate from power and ignore an essential part of himself, his hereditary right and duty? It seems from his words that this is exactly his aim. Duty is to be sacrificed for enjoyment:

> And now, thou ceremonious sovereignty,
> Ye proud, severer, stateful complements,
> The secret arts of rule, I put you off;
> Nor ever shall those manacles of form
> Once more lock up the appetite of blood.
> 'Tis now an age of man, whilst we all strict
> Have liv'd in awe of carriage regular
> Apted unto my place, nor hath my life
> Once tasted of exorbitant affects,
> Wild longings, or the least of disrank'd shapes.
> But we must once be wild, 'tis ancient truth.
> O fortunate, whose madness falls in youth!
>
> (*The Fawn*, I. i. 36–47)[20]

Kantorowicz[21] has well documented an Elizabethan belief that an ordained prince could not commit an act of apostasy against his kingship, whether he did this intentionally or by the force of others. Kingship being an indivisible part of himself meant that only death could proffer release. But, alternatively, as plays such as *Henry IV*, *Henry V*, *As You Like It* and Rowley's *When You See Me You Know Me* illustrate, the idea of reversal of roles, or, at least, the incognito visit conducted so as to enhance a prince's wisdom through at what might first appear to be folly, was accepted as perfectly satisfactory conduct. Hercules's act of foolishness at the beginning of *The Fawn* is soon stated unequivocally to be within this latter tradition. It has a twin motive. First, by briefly reversing his role he may learn how to become a better ruler. Secondly, through watching his son's conduct he hopes to discover how his plan to secure the line of succession – through either himself or Tiberio marrying the princess – will fare.[22] These two motives jointly give the play its structure and place it within its comic convention.

To be a good ruler one must follow the dictates of one's own nature, as prince and man. When a prince you have to behave as a prince but not allow the opinion of others to let you forget your manhood:

> Shall I because some few may cry, 'Light, vain,'
> Beat down affection from desired rule
> (He that doth strive to please the world's a fool),
> To have that fellow cry, 'O mark him, grave,
> See how austerely he doth give example
> Of repressed heat and steady life,'
> Whilst my forc'd life against the stream of blood
> Is tugg'd along, and all to keep the God
> Of fools and men: nice opinion,
> Whose strict preserving makes oft great men fools
> And fools oft great men.
>
> (I. i. 50–60)

Thematically these statements in Act I serve as a contrast to the conduct of Duke Gonzago. By not relaxing his role as 'wise' duke, Gonzago makes himself the fool of the play, whilst Hercules, by adhering to the tradition of humiliation – exemplified as an underlying concept of the Feast of Fools – becomes the wise man. No sooner has Hercules become Faunus than he begins to learn the wisdom that both Henry V and Henry VIII learnt:

> I never knew till now how old I was.
> By Him by Whom we are, I think a prince
> Whose tender sufferance never felt a gust
> Of bolder breathings, but still liv'd gently fann'd
> With the soft gales of his own flatterers' lips,
> Shall never know his own complexion.
> Dear sleep and lust, I thank you. But for you,
> Mortal till now, I scarce had known myself.
>
> (I. ii. 305–12)

Self-revelation soon beginning to be learnt, but with the duke still in disguise, Hercules is now able to use his conscious folly to cure the subconscious foolishness at Gonzago's court. He is able to become a critic–commentator of the type found in Marston's earlier plays, but this time, because the inconsistency between the true identity and the role has been adequately defined early in the play, we have no doubt of the direction in which his satire is to be carried. We know that he is in total control of the situation, and that no other character will have the wisdom to challenge his position, since all others, except Dulcimel, are blinded by their own natural folly. Hercules's knowledge of his situation in comparison with that of Gonzago and his courtiers places him in an unassailable position. Kaplan has perceptively realised the significance and exact nature of this situation. Hercules combines elements of both the satiric and the saturnalian. Marston's references, throughout his poems and plays, to the classical Hercules reveal that he was particularly interested in two actions performed by the hero: the 'cleansing of the Augean stables', and the 'apocryphal thirteenth labor, the impregnation of King Thespius's fifty daughters in a single night'. Thus,

> For Marston . . . the [Classical] figure of Hercules, first at the Augean stalls and then in the bedrooms of Beotia, was associated with both the carting of filth and the creation of progeny. Appropriately these acts are, in the broadest sense of the terms, the respective domains of renaissance satire and comedy; the realms of the satirist and what we may call the saturnalian character.

The name of Duke Hercules is not fortuitous, since 'Marston's Duke Hercules fulfills both functions. He is at the same time a satiric and saturnalian figure, cleansing Gonzago's polluted court at Urbin while perpetuating his own house at Ferrara.'[23] This is exactly the strength of the character. Saturnalian certainly in the reversal of his role-play so as to discover and purge his own folly, Duke Hercules is able to be satiric about others who have not followed his example. The result is that he appears as a strongly defined character having a positive approach to his role, in contrast with, for example, Malevole, who because of a loss of identity wanders about his dukedom searching for himself. Yet it is this definition in character which largely accounts for the lightness and gaiety of *The Fawn*, in similar contrast to the rather austere but deeper comic significance that we found in *The Malcontent*.

Within the context of the Hercules twin motives, the matrimonial situation is developed to provide a stronger narrative line than the Celia–Albano story in *What You Will*. As a firm central story it serves as a means by which all the minor comic episodes may be focused and it relieves some of the burden from the figure of critic–commentator as the main unifying force of the drama. Nevertheless, Marston's artistry at creating entertainment through cleverly designed individual episodes is still evident in the play. A clear example of this is found in the satiric portrait of Don Zuccone in Act II, scene i. This highlights the tenuous line between sublimity and the grotesque, pride and its fall, whilst being thematically connected to a central issue of the play, the relationship of man and woman. By striving for a role which is divorced from human nature, Zuccone creates a false picture of himself which can be seen by all. This becomes more evident when we attempt to reconstruct the scene as it might be performed. In Act II, scene i, Zuccone enters upstage right, with pompous dignity. Downstage left, Herod and Hercules are in conversation, Nymphadoro and Sir Amoroso near them. Herod immediately undercuts the picture of the Don by describing him as an 'egregious idiot' and by telling us that there is a comic plot to be enacted against him. Nymphadoro breaks from the group and encounters Zuccone about centre right. Zuccone in his indifference can hardly be bothered to answer, but as he does so he establishes himself as the centre of our attention.

Nymphadoro	A quiet bosom to my sweet Don. Are you going to visit your lady?
Zuccone	What o'clock is't? Is it past three?
Herod	Past four, I assure you, sweet Don.
Zuccone	O, then, I may be admitted; her afternoon's private nap is taken. I shall take her napping. I hear there's one jealous that I lie with my own wife, and begins to withdraw his hand. I protest, I vow – and you will, on my knees I'll take my sacrament on it – I lay not with her this four year, this four year. Let her not be turn'd upon me, I beseech you.

(II. i. 197–206)

Hercules, plainly ready to enjoy and help the fun of Herod's plot, moves away from Herod and greets the Don centre stage – 'My dear Don!' – leading him away, centre right. Zuccone goes with him, whilst Nymphadoro returns centre left. Thinking that he is totally in control of the picture he presents to himself and the world, Zuccone continues to boast of his wisdom both to Hercules and across the stage to Nymphadoro and Herod. We can imagine Zuccone with silks and perfume and a handkerchief hanging from his sleeve. Suddenly his visual antithesis, 'the bald fool' Dondolo, runs on from the tiring-house upstage right. He rushes to each character, pushing through Amoroso and Nymphadoro, greeting them and Herod on the way, and then crossing down stage to Hercules and finally the Don. 'News, news, news, news! O, my dear Don, be rais'd, be jovial, be triumphant, ah, my dear Don' (II. i. 224–5). It takes only these few words to unsettle Zuccone's image of himself by raising curiosity, but the artistry of the scene now becomes apparent as Nymphadoro, having followed Dondolo across stage, leads him away from Zuccone, down right.

Nymphadoro	To me first in private, thy news, I prithee.
Dondolo	Will you be secret?
Nymphadoro	O' my life.
Dondolo	As you are generous?
Nymphadoro	As I am generous.

(II. i. 226–30)

Obviously this part of the conversation is conducted with enough volume for Zuccone's ears, but then at the crucial moment Dondolo takes Nymphadoro one step further away from Zuccone and whispers the exact matter: 'Don Zuccone's lady's with child'. Zuccone's frustration is increased, but the role he has acquired demands that he continues seemingly to keep his composure. He hovers about centre stage as Herod calls Nymphadoro across to him, down left. Zuccone's eyes follow him across stage, but he remains where he is whilst the news is again given out of his hearing. Nymphadoro, having given his message to Hercules, rushes to Sir Amoroso up stage and quietly tells him, whilst Hercules loudly whispers across stage to Herod, 'Herod, Herod, what's the matter prithee? The news?' Herod looks at Zuccone and then back to Hercules to whom he says 'you must tell nobody' and calls Hercules over to him; Zuccone's eyes following once again. The news is given. Zuccone, his curiosity raised to breaking-point, with desperation approaches Hercules, who having heard the news moves centre left. 'Fawn, what's the whisper? What's the fool's secret news?' Hercules maintains the game, 'Truth, my lord, a thing, that, that – well, i'faith, it is not fit you know it.' He moves away from him downstage centre. Zuccone follows, 'Not fit I know it? As thou art baptiz'd tell me, tell me.' Hercules looks around the stage to make sure no one will hear and takes Zuccone by the arm. The whole situation is absurd in its humour:

Hercules	Will you plight your patience to it?
Zuccone	Speak, I am a very block. I will not be mov'd. I am a very block.
Hercules	But if you should grow disquiet (as I protest, it would make a saint blaspheme), I should be unwilling to procure your impatience.
Zuccone	Yes, do, burst me, burst me, burst me with longing.

Hercules	Nay, faith, 'tis no great matter. Hark ye, you'll tell nobody?
Zuccone	Not.

(II. i. 244–52)

All the other characters now watch delighted with expectation, as does the audience, to see the result of the joke; their suspense almost matching that of Zuccone himself. Hercules begins to move even further down stage and to the right, Zuccone continuing to follow:

Hercules	As you are noble?
Zuccone	As I am honest.
Hercules	Your lady wife is apparently with child.
Zuccone	With child?
Hercules	With child.
Zuccone	Fool!
Hercules	My Don.

(II. i. 253–9)

Hercules immediately leaves Zuccone alone downstage right and returns left to the group, who in the meantime have been joined by Dondolo. They all wait for the penny to drop. Zuccone thinks for a while. There is a pause and then: 'With child! By the pleasure of generation, I proclaim I lay not with her this – give us patience, give us patience. . . .' The penny drops. His sublimity through agitation falls to a grotesque grimace as Herod, Hercules and the rest move in for the comic kill. Eventually he pushes past them all and in confused anger leaves the stage:

> Do not anger me, lest I most dreadfully curse thee, and wish thee married. O, Zuccone, spit white, spit thy gall out. The only boon I crave of heaven is – but to have my honors inherited by a bastard! I will be most tyrannous, bloodily tyrannous in my revenge, and most terrible in my curses. Live to grow blind with lust, senseless with use, loathed after, flattered before, hated always, trusted never, abhorred ever, and last may she live to wear a foul smock seven weeks together, heaven, I beseech thee!
>
> (II. i. 285–93)

This is one possible interpretation of the comic activity that is implicit in this finely drawn ground-plan for a scene. The scene, one of many similarly drawn episodes in the play, shows Marston's comic artistry at its height. The deflátion of folly, the exaggeration of caricature, the impetus for movement, agitation, suspense and rage all combine within a small satiric picture to produce a total comic effect. Yet the actual matter of the comedy has related to the overall love theme of the play. Zuccone's humiliation is only a variation on that to be experienced by Gonzago, Herod and the others sentenced later to the ship of fools, in contrast to the naturalness of the Tiberio–Dulcimel relationship.

Written after *Jack Drum*, *The Malcontent*, *What You Will* and *The Dutch Courtesan*, *The Fawn*, though a slighter play in theme than two of these, must be seen in the context of Marston's development in artistry. It is surprising that in the past critics have not given it the attention that it demands, since of all the plays it seems to be technically the most sound. Audience expectations are not frustrated; the character of the central satiric figure – unlike Quadratus, Freevill, and Malevole – is clearly defined; the relationship between the comic episode and an overall theme – unlike in *Jack Drum* – is consistent. On stage the scenes develop with great comic skill, and within the comic and satiric romance convention they would provide in performance, as we have seen, great entertainment. Consequently it is regrettable that the play has received no major dramatic revival in England this century. Perhaps this is just for economic reasons, or perhaps directors, in not finding Hercules as interesting and ambiguous a figure as Malevole or Freevill, have not explored the comic possibilities inherent in the farce. The latter is certainly one of the ironic reasons why *The Fawn* cannot be classed as one of Marston's major works. But, whatever the reasons, it seems that, although technically superior[24] to *Jack Drum* and *What You Will*, *The Fawn* is to remain in their company, classified by the critic as a good entertainment but sentenced to live in the dramatic obscurity of the written page, locked away in the 'cedar chests' of Marston's preface to the play. Yet it is in a postscript to that same preface that Marston again reminds us of his purpose in writing: 'Comedies are writ to be spoken, not read. Remember the life of these things consists in action. . . .' It is unfortunate that, for the moment, the comedy of *The Fawn* can live only in our imagination.

6
Language and Theme

Much of *The Fawn* is about language; its use and abuse at court. If, as Jonson held, 'Language most shewes the man; speake that I may see thee', what language shows us in *The Fawn* is a gallery of fops and fools in love with sound but ignorant of meaning. In Act I Duke Hercules, plainly influenced by Montaigne, dreams of the alternative to this situation:

> Most spotless kingdom,
> And men, O happy born under good stars,
> Where what is honest you may freely think,
> Speak what you think, and write what you do speak,
> Not bound to servile soothings.
>
> (*The Fawn*, I. ii. 319–23)

His solution is to follow a form of comic reversal. He has already declared his intention of following the freedom of nature rather than 'nice opinion' (I. i. 47–61) but makes the further decision to flatter all:

> In all of their extremest viciousness,
> Till in their own lov'd race they fall most lame,
> And meet full butt the close of vice's shame.
>
> (I. ii. 335–7)

He becomes as affected as the rest but has the advantage throughout of consciously acting the fop rather than being the fool. Consequently all his flattery is designed to expose the truths behind the false language of characters such as Herod:

Hercules Come, what are you fleering at? There's some weakness in your brother you wrinkle at thus. Come, prithee impart. What? We are mutually incorporated, turn'd one into another, brewed together. Come, I believe you are familiar with your sister, and it were known.

Herod Witch, Faunus, witch. Why, how dost dream I live? Is't fourscore a year, thinkst thou, maintains my geldings, my pages, foot-cloths, my best feeding, high play, and excellent company? No, 'tis from hence, from hence, I mint some four hundred pound a year.

Hercules Dost thou live like a porter, by thy back, boy? . . . Dost thou branch him, boy?

Herod What else, Fawn?

(II. i. 162–72, 178–9)

Unlike Malevole, Hercules does not rant at his opponents but rather imitates their linguistic manner. He becomes jovial with them and associates himself with their deeds, thus encouraging their pride. Consequently he gains their trust and in response they tell him their vices and follies, real or fictitious, since they believe he will be impressed by what they consider to be their 'accomplishments'. It is therefore the manner of his imitative and pandering speech which becomes the cornerstone of Hercules's success: an act which he perfects to such an extent that he can even tell Herod exactly what he thinks of him, without Herod taking offence or even realising that the truth is being spoken:

Hercules What else? Nay, 'tis enough. Why, many men corrupt other men's wives, some their maids, others their neighbors' daughters, but to lie with one's brother's wedlock, O, my dear Herod, 'tis vile and common lust.

Herod 'Fore heaven, I love thee to the heart. Well, I may praise God for my brother's weakness, for I assure thee, the land shall descend to me, my little Fawn.

Hercules To thee, my little Herod? O my rare rascal, I do find more and more in thee to wonder at, for thou art indeed – if I prosper, thou shalt know what.

(II. i. 180–9)

Herod, too puffed up with his own importance, cannot see irony or double meanings in what Hercules says. He takes it all as it sounds, since superficiality flatters.

The fundamental problem with Herod, Gonzago, Nymphadoro and their companions is that they think they speak and hear so clearly. Gonzago, the worst offender, judges all his statements by a mistaken notion of bookish eloquence. His language is such that in his 'well experienced age' he knows himself to be 'the true Delphos' (I. ii. 150). Rhetorically he denies his use of rhetoric (I. ii. 185) but later lets all know that he has read *'Cicero de Oratore'* (IV. i. 584). When his daughter mockingly imitates his manner of speech he shows pride, reflecting 'that eloquence is hereditary' (III. i. 325). Language at this court therefore is being employed not for communication but for the exultation of self. In the conclusion it is exposed as such by Hercules, particularly when he ridicules Granuffo, the man who has the conceit to think himself above language itself:

Hercules	'An act against mummers, false seemers, that abuse ladies with counterfeit faces, courting only by signs, and seeming wise only by silence.'
Cupid	The penalty?
Hercules	To be urged to speak, and then, if inward ability answer not outward seeming, to be committed instantly to the ship of fools during great Cupid's pleasure. – My Lord Granuffo, to the bar! Speak, speak, is not this law just?
Granuffo	Just, sure; for in good truth or in good sooth, When wise men speak, they still must open their mouth.
Hercules	The brazen head has spoken.
Dondolo	Thou art arrested.
Granuffo	Me?
Hercules	And judg'd. Away!

(v. i. 353–66)

Language seems to be a central concern not only in *The Fawn* but in most of Marston's works,[1] and yet, ironically, from the first appearance of the plays, it has been his use of dramatic language that has received most condemnation from critics. In *The Poetàster*, Act v, scene iii, Jonson provided him with a linguistic purge to rid him of such 'windie wordes' as 'magnificate', 'spurious snotteries', 'childblain'd', 'clumsie', 'barmy froth', 'puffy', 'inflate', 'turgidous', and 'ventositous'. In our own century Theodore Spencer represents the long tradition of similar criticism:

> Marston knew what *ought* to be said, but his sensitivity was only half-developed; he knew the analytical meaning of words, but was unaware of their connotations; as a result his poetry is dry, it lacks overtones, it walks unnaturally on stilts, and only very rarely does it give the impression of ease and control which we find in [the] poetry . . . [of] Dante and Shakespeare: 'As having clasp'd a rose / Within my palm, the rose being ta'en away / My hand retains a little breath of sweet . . .' Lines like these are exceptional in Marston: they seem to have slipped out accidentally, before he had time to spoil them by overloading them with heavy adjectives.[2]

Such criticisms arise from a misconception about the way Marston employed words, and the habit of measuring drama with a literary yardstick. Even when Marston passages have been praised by critics such as Lamb, in his admiration of the prologue to *Antonio's Revenge*,[3] or by Spencer, in the brief quotation above, the praise has been given because some individual passages may be compared with the verse of a great poet. Lamb cites Milton, Spencer recalls Dante and Shakespeare. Yet the passages quoted, as Spencer notes, are 'exceptional'. The trouble has been that critics have largely ignored Marston's repeated requests for his plays to be seen rather than read and have consequently judged him by their own misconceived ideas about the 'literariness' of dramatic language.

Fortunately there has been, as we have noted, a reaction against such approaches to dramatic language. Terence Hawkes, for example, following men of the theatre such as Gordon Craig and Arthur Miller, has pointed out that there is more to a play than its words:

> Drama, in short, is made out of language. Acting is a stylization of linguistic 'interacting'. It depends, as communication outside the theatre does, on a good deal more than words set in the 'grammatical' patterns appropriate to writing and the literary notion of 'text'.
>
> In fact, of all forms of art in which societies engage, drama remains the only one which wholly derives from and fully exploits the 'central fact' of man's 'talking' nature. In general terms, drama celebrates, manifests, and is 'about' the complex reality of man as the 'talking animal'. In particular, it draws upon the full range of verbal and non-verbal activities involved in 'talking'.[4]

If we are to understand Marston's use of verbal language it is necessary therefore to see it in the context of the dramatic conduct of the plays themselves. Such an approach, as Una Ellis Fermor pointed out, reveals one of his major strengths:

> For it is Marston who, when the spasmodic and undisciplined hyperbole of his early vocabulary is reduced (whether by the ministrations of Ben Jonson or by the milder operations of time and natural development), maintains by the strength and daring of his imagery the tragic tradition of Marlowe and of Shakespeare's early work, confirming imagery as a vital and integral part of dramatic expression, conferring upon it a function which no major dramatist of the succeeding decade disregarded, that of supplying the essential indications of mood and underlying thought without which neither plot, character nor the true aesthetic values of the play could be rightly apprehended.[5]

Our reaction to Marston's verbal language, therefore, should be coloured not so much by the judgement of its intrinsic poetic or literary merit as by its relevance to the play and situation in which it occurs.

In terms of English drama, Jonson's statement that language denotes the man was not very original. When Marston employed eccentricities and abuses of language to illustrate character and theme he was following a long tradition. Language for the medieval dramatists was often seen as a means of indicating the nature of the speaker. In *Mundus et Infans* (c. 1508), for example, the different ages of man have an appropriate rhythmic line. Whereas the youth of the boy is expressed by a skipping short rhythm, the metre is extended as he grows to manhood.[6] The line itself becomes longer, slower and more masculine. Similarly, in *Enough Is as Good as a Feast* (c. 1560), the vice figure is denoted by the illogicality of his language:

At Blackheath field, where great Goliath was slain,
The Moon lying in childbed of her last son,
The Tyburn at Warwick was then King of Spain,
By whom the Land of Canaan then was won.
It happened between Peterborough and Pentecost,
About such time as Ivy was made of Wormwood,
That Child's work in Basil wood of fire was lost,
And all through the treason of false Robin Hood.
That saw Sir Guy of Warwick and Colebrand,
Which fought against the sun and stopped his light.
'Yea,' quoth Hobgoblin, 'let me take them in hand –
Children, children not able to resist my might!'[7]

The passage is seemingly nonsensical, but spoken out it gives the sound of sense. Rhymes, alliteration, changes of tone are all present. The figure speaking is Covetous and the manner of his speech reveals his nature as the vice; evil sounds good but in actuality is empty and absurd. Talking of the twentieth-century movement of absurd theatre, Peter Brook points to the new vocabulary that has been introduced by 'using language illogically' and by 'introducing the ridiculous in speech and the fantastic in behaviour'.[8] Marston, capitalising on a medieval tradition of word and manner of speech denoting character and theme, often combines both these elements, the ridiculous and the fantastic. We find, in fact, elements of what Brook calls 'a language of sounds – a language of word-as-part-of-movement, of word-as-lie, word-as-parody, of word-as-rubbish, of word-as-contradiction, of word-shock . . . word-cry'.[9] Hunter has already noted the almost absurd conversation that occurs between Balurdo and Feliche early in the last act of *Antonio and Mellida*:

Feliche	Now, Master Balurdo, whither are you going, ha?
Balurdo	Signior Feliche, how do you, faith, and by my troth, how do you?
Feliche	Whither are thou going, bully?
Balurdo	And as heaven help me, how do you? How do you i'faith, hee?
Feliche	Whither art going man?

(*A & M*, v. i. 67–73)

Both characters are so involved with their own self, with their own interests, that communication is lost: questions are asked but not heard, sounds are made without sense. We find similar instances, as we have seen, throughout *The Fawn*, where, in particular, 'word-as-parody' is employed. In many of the plays, however, Marston accomplishes the same effect by giving his characters speech impediments, often a stutter or a foreign accent. The comedy of *Jack Drum's Entertainment* is increased by the introduction of the mispronunciations of the fool lover John fo de King. But more important is Franceschina's heavy accent in *The Dutch Courtesan*, since it is a dramatic device employed to isolate her on stage, thus emphasising her lack of integration into society. Malevole, similarly, employs 'word-as-contradiction' and 'word-shock' to illustrate his position as the outsider of a corrupt society. Throughout the *Antonio* plays the disruption of rationality and the excesses of passion, as noted earlier, are continually emphasised by characters' losing the power of coherent speech. The device is seen again in *What You Will* where Albano, unable to relate himself to the situation created by others, falls victim to an uncontrollable stutter:

Albano	A fiddler, a scraper, a miniken tickler, a pum, a pum, even now a Perfumer, now a fiddler, I will be even *What you will*, do, do, do, k, k, k, kisse my wife be, be, be, be, fore –
Quadratus	Why would'st have him kisse her behind?
Albano	Before my own f, f, f, face.
Iacomo	Well done fiddler!
Albano	Ile f, f, fiddle yee.

(*What You Will*, p. 282)

Perhaps the most interesting example of many of these devices throughout the *Antonio* plays is found in the figure of Balurdo. By constantly reducing language to the banal, Balurdo stands as the mean of the linguistic confusion which in one way or another is prevalent in all the characters of the two plays. Consequently his misuse of language signified by his very first words 'O, I smell a sound' (*A & M*, I. i. 43) symbolises and reflects the disorientation and disorder of the society in which he lives. The control of language in Piero's Venice is the means by which power, tyranny or safety are decided. It is Andrugio's clever interpretation of Piero's vow at the end of *Antonio and Mellida* which preserves his life. It is Antonio's action of 'seizing' Piero's 'breath' in the same scene which restores him to his Mellida, and it is Piero's dissembling that perpetrates the atrocities at the beginning of *Antonio's Revenge*. Truth is divorced from language throughout, so that normal words no longer mean anything. Balurdo is constantly striving to be held in good grace by the court, but he cannot control the courtiers' 'eloquence'. Language becomes an obsession with him. He notes new words, 'propitious', 'retort', 'obtuse', and, within the Renaissance tradition of this kind of clown (who is commonly used as a satire on the inkhornists), he is continually seen preening himself with the pretensions of expression:

Balurdo 'Now nimble wits appear': I'll myself appear;
Balurdo's self, that in quick wit doth surpass,
Will show the substance of a complete –
Dildo Ass, Ass.
Balurdo I'll mount my courser and most gallantly prick –
Dildo 'Gallantly prick' is too long, and stands hardly in the verse, sir.
Balurdo I'll speak pure rhyme and will so bravely prank it
That I'll toss love like a – prank – prank it – a rhyme for 'prank it'?
Dildo Blanket.
Balurdo That I'll toss love like a dog in a blanket. Ha, ha, indeed, la; I think – ha, ha, I think – ha, ha, I think I shall tickle the Muses. And I strike it not dead, say, 'Balurdo, thou art an arrant sot.'
Dildo Balurdo, thou art an arrant sot.

(*A & M*, IV. i. 264–79)

Even the fool, Dildo, ridicules his linguistic aspirations and shows more knowledge of such linguistic matters as innuendo and ambiguity. Consequently it comes as no surprise when Balurdo tells of his 'monstrous strange dream':

methought I dream'd I was asleep, and methought the ground

yawn'd and belk'd up the abominable ghost of a misshapen Simile, with two ugly pages, the one called Master *Even-as*, going before, and the other Mounser *Even-so*, following after, whilst Signior Simile stalked most prodigiously in the midst. At which I bewrayed the fearfulness of my nature, and (being ready to forsake the fortress of my wit) start up, called for a clean shirt, eat a mess of broth, and with that I awak'd.

(*AR*, I. i. 126–34)

In reality, however, the pathetically innocent Balurdo never does wake. He cannot conceive of Piero's verbal dexterities and dissimulations which dominate the play, and thus he may be seen to be in almost a different world from the Duke. Ironically, therefore, it is his banality which betrays his innocence in comparison with others' degeneration. He dreams of similes because he cannot control them, but it is this lack of linguistic power which provides him with an endearing quality and defines his role in the work. His words on seeing the 'dead' Antonio in *Antonio and Mellida* by their simplicity emphasise for the audience the preceding emptiness of Piero's eloquence:

Piero O that my tears bedewing thy wan cheek
Could make new spirit sprout in thy cold blood.
Balurdo Verily, he looks as pitifully as a poor John; as I am a true knight, I could weep like a ston'd horse.

(*A & M*, V. ii. 199–202)

His words are similarly juxtaposed with Piero's in *Antonio's Revenge* when Maria faints on hearing of Andrugio's death:

Piero Be cheerful, princess; help, Castilio,
The lady's swooned; help to bear her in.
Slow comfort to huge cares is swiftest sin.
Balurdo Courage, courage, sweet lady; 'tis Sir Jeffrey Balurdo bids you courage. Truly, I am as nimble as an elephant about a lady.

(*AR*, I. ii. 250–5)

In the end, too, it is this mixture of honesty and a desire to be heard and acknowledged which in *Antonio's Revenge*, Act IV, scene ii, leads him into prison. For all his 'go to's Balurdo retains a certain integrity behind his attempted eloquence and abortive efforts to be highly regarded by the Duke.

If Balurdo is constantly trying to be acknowledged by Piero's society, Antonio and Mellida are continually attempting to make their escape. But as with Balurdo it is their language which reflects their significance in the dramatic theme. Critics have been totally perplexed by the linguistic conduct of the lovers' scene in *Antonio and Mellida*, Act IV, scene i. Swinburne summarised the problem:

> The brief fourth act of 'Antonio and Mellida' is the most astonishing and bewildering production of belated human genius that ever distracted or discomforted a student. Verses more delicately beautiful followed by verses more simply majestic than these [IV. i. 13–23] have rarely if ever given assurance of eternity to the fame of any but a great master in song. . . . Then follows a passage of sheer gibberish; then a dialogue of the noblest and most dramatic eloquence; then a chaotic alternation of sense and nonsense, bad Italian and mixed English, abject farce and dignified rhetoric, spirited simplicity and bombastic jargon. It would be more and less than just to take this act as a sample or a symbol of the author's usual way of work, but I cannot imagine that a parallel to it, for evil or for good, could be found in the works of any other writer.[10]

The same scene and particularly the Italian also troubled T. S. Eliot: 'it is difficult to explain, by any natural action of mediocrity the absurd dialogue in Italian in which Antonio and Mellida suddenly express themselves'.[11] Yet, if, as we have seen with Balurdo, language is a criterion whereby we judge social reality, the confusion, the gibberish, the Italian, the 'word-as-[seemingly]-rubbish' may be justified. First, the juxtaposing of gross linguistic mannerisms, accompanied by the appropriate melodramatic gestures, adds to the over-all humour and tenor of the play; but, secondly, through satire, these mannerisms and gestures serve as comment on the nature of the court and on social conventions and attitudes in general. Antonio's despair at losing Mellida (*A & M*, IV. i. 23–8) is ridiculed, as we have seen, by aposiopesis,[12] but his joy at finding her is similarly satirised through the Italian dialogue. Marston here emphasises the nature and excesses of romantic love. What seems more foolish to disinterested outsiders than the ridiculous professions of faith of a loving couple? Lovers are foolish animals to all but themselves,[13] and thus at the end of this humorous dialogue the page remains on the stage to comment:

> I think confusion of Babel is fall'n upon these lovers, that they change their language; but I fear me my master, having but feigned the person of a woman, hath got their unfeigned imperfection and is grown double tongu'd. As for Mellida, she were no woman if she could not yield strange language. But howsoever, if

> I should sit in judgement, 'tis an error easier to be pardoned by the auditors' than excused by the author's; and yet some private respect may rebate the edge of the keener censure.
>
> (*A & M*, IV. i. 219–27)

Through the page Marston asks us to reflect on a scene which at first appearance might seem absurd. The 'edge of keener censure' is somewhat dulled when we consider that not only is a comic effect being aimed at here but also a necessary statement concerning the lovers is being proposed. Love can separate the participants from the society to which they usually belong – a separation which in the context of the Venetian court is a more than happy release. If there is any linguistic truth in the *Antonio* plays, besides Balurdo's simplicity, it is in the incomprehensible and extreme Italian. The absurd lapse into the language isolates the lovers from the dissimulation of Piero's court. It also shows the nature of the lovers who 'think the same thoughts without the need of speech / And babble the same speech without the need of meaning'.[14] The scene is an example of Marston's dual perspective. It at once isolates the lovers in their own world and produces our laughter. Combined, the two partly illustrate the nature of his satiric purpose.[15]

A similar argument may be made for his seemingly continued preoccupation 'with the waste products of the body, with vomit and spit, sweat and excrement, abscesses and putrefaction'.[16] Commentators have been prone to see this imagery as reflecting dubious moral attitudes in the dramatist himself, but in doing so have fallen into the trap of equating characters and symbols with the personality of the author.

In the same way that language depicts the man, so it can express the nature of inanimate ideas such as lust, sycophancy and tyranny. It is in this sphere probably more than anywhere that Marston employed poetic effects as a dramatic instrument. Poetic description need not necessarily be confined to objects for admiration or for characters facing moral dilemmas. There is no necessary relationship between verse and beauty, as, for example, Spenser's disrobing of Duessa illustrates. Thus there should be few objections to Marston's technique of describing the evils he is exposing with all the necessary descriptive power that he can muster. Consequently we find in *Sophonisba* Syphax's enthusiastic description of Erictho, the symbol of his own lust:

> A loathsome yellowe leannesse spreades hir face
> A heavy hell-like palenes loades hir cheekes
> Unknowne to a cleare heaven . . .
> but when she findes a corse

New gravd whose entrailes yet not turne
To slymy filth with greedy havock then
She makes fierce spoile: & swels with wicked triumph
To bury hir leane knuckles in his eyes
Then doeth she knaw the pale and or'egrowne nailes
From his dry hand: but if she find some life
Yet lurking close she bites his gelled lips,
And sticking her blacke tongue in his drie throat,
She breathes dire murmurs, which inforce him beare
Her banefull secrets to the spirits of horror.

(*Sophonisba*, pp. 46–7)

This is a lingering, horrific and sensual description of the final degradation accompanying lust. The language is foul, but is only as disgusting as the murder of Julio in *Antonio's Revenge*, the Thyestean banquet of *Titus Andronicus*, or the blinding of Gloucester in *King Lear*. Lust is the moral disease of which Syphax is the hopeless victim. He consequently conjures up the witch and talks about her with almost ecstatic excitement. His imagination is captivated and dwells therefore on her nature with an enthusiasm and a leering sensuality. Such is the reality of the sin. It envelops the whole of man; it excites him; it encourages his enthusiasm; it stimulates his sensual imagination; it possesses him. Syphax's poetry is necessarily detailed in its perverted sexuality. He dwells on the repulsive as if it were attractive. The effect is to horrify and repulse the audience. We are simultaneously presented with a verbal portrait of the foul witch and made fully aware of how the illusion of lust can cause a man to fall under her spell. Marston is brilliantly describing the evil to us in all its facets, but he does this not only by the horrific imagery but also by creating a character, Syphax, who at one and the same time draws, and is part of, the horrific picture presented. The language must be seen in the context of the way it is delivered, its position in the play and the total dramatic situation.

With such pictures Marston is attempting to describe the true nature of his characters' experiences. Thus when, in *Antonio's Revenge*, Pandulpho asks Piero 'Why taint'st thou then the air with stench of flesh / And human putrefaction's noisome scent?' (*AR*, II. i. 67–8) – a question to which Samuel Schoenbaum takes exception – he is attempting to make the audience realise the full significance of what is happening in the play. Feliche's body has been hanging from the walls 'stabbed thick with wounds' for most of the drama. It is an important reminder of the horrific reality of Piero's court. Feliche has been murdered, his reputation abused and the corpse exposed. The visual symbol is complemented therefore by the language of Pandulpho. We, as audience, cannot smell the rotting body, so the sense impression is described to us. Here is no obscure fiction but the repulsive reality of pseudo-Machiavellian politics. The language consequently is an instrument of the dramatic intent. It exposes rather than conceals, since that is the purpose of the bitter dramatist, especially one influenced by Montaigne:

> For my part I am resolved to dare speake whatsoever I dare do: And am displeased with thoughts not to be published. The worst of my actions or condicions seeme not so ugly unto me, as I finde it both ugly and base not to dare to avouch them. . . . He that should be bound to tell all, should also bind himselfe to do nothing which one is forced to conceale.[17]

Marston's work illustrates that he believed the same might be said of society. His verbal language, far from showing a moral ambivalence, aids a dramatic purpose of exposure and ridicule, and does so to a remarkable extent.

7 Dreams, Innovation and Technique

In *The Empty Space* (p. 87) Peter Brook writes,

> The exchange of impressions through images is our basic language: at the moment when one man expresses an image at that same instant the other man meets him in belief. The shared association is the language: if the association evokes nothing in the second person, if there is no instant of shared illusion, there is no exchange.

Marston was a major figure in moving towards the creation of the total dramatic image: the language not only of words but also of sounds, actions and dreams. It is possible to identify two major conventions employed in his compositions; the episodic and the linear. The former is exemplified by *What You Will*; the latter by *Sophonisba*. But it would be a mistake even to attempt to categorise each play under one or other of these headings. The dramas show that Marston, like Marlowe, Shakespeare and Jonson, was constantly experimenting with his dramatic form, its conventions and techniques. Elements of *Tamburlaine*, *Volpone* and *Hamlet* may be seen during the development of his art, but in his most successful plays we discover an innovatory technique which has led Hunter to proclaim him as 'the most modern of the Elizabethans'.[1]

At the point of anagnorisis in *The Malcontent* the dismayed Mendoza, seeing his defeat, cries out,

> Are we surprised? What strange delusions mock
> Our senses? Do I dream? or have I dreamt
> This two days' space? Where am I?
>
> (*The Malcontent*, v. vi. 117–19)

Similarly Gonzago, recognising Hercules and his own folly in *The Fawn*, reflects, 'By the Lord, I am asham'd of myself, that's the plain troth. But I know now wherefore this parliament was. What a slumber I have been in!' (*The Fawn*, v. i. 452–4). Mendoza and

Gonzago therefore admit to having been living in a world of illusion. Both men have been deluded into thinking that they controlled the conduct of the narrative, but have finally realised that throughout they did not possess the necessary wisdom or information to have any effect on the proceedings. Their dream worlds have been their illusions of power, or of wisdom. Likewise, as we have seen, Syphax in *Sophonisba* makes dream fantasy a temporary reality when he sleeps with the witch but awakens to the full horror of his lust:

> Thou rotten scum of Hell –
> O my abhorred heat! O loath'd delusion!
> (*Sophonisba*, p. 51)

It is from this dream stance that we may look at the satiric drama to see how Marston's dramatic techniques complemented narrative material. The convention of the dream may be seen in two ways. First, there is the idea that the characters involved in the plays are in a dream situation; and, secondly, Marston may have considered that the audience can be regarded as similarly in a dream situation in experiencing a dramatic performance.

It is not merely Mendoza in *The Malcontent* who is acknowledged to have been a participant in a dream. The satiric language of Malevole emphasises that the conduct of the court is as one long nightmare:

> Pietro — How dost spend the night? I hear thou never sleep'st.
> Malevole — O, no, but dream the most fantastical . . . O heaven! O fubbery, fubbery!
> Pietro — Dream! what dreamest?
> Malevole — Why, methinks I see that signior pawn his footcloth, that metreza her plate; this madam takes physic, that t'other monsieur may minister to her; here is a pander jewelled; there is a fellow in shift of satin this day, that could not shift a shirt t'other night. Here a Paris supports that Helen; there's a Lady Guinever bears up that Sir Lancelot – dreams, visions, fantasies, chimeras, imaginations, tricks, conceits!
> (*The Malcontent*, I. iii. 45–56)

Malevole cannot sleep, as he tells us again in his soliloquy at III. ii. 1–14, but he can still talk of dreams, since the whole courtly world is one of people's illusions and fantasies. They all think that they are fulfilling their lives; but the malcontent, the outsider, can from his objective position see and understand their self-deception. The same is true of Hercules in *The Fawn*. As we have seen, it is not until he dissociates himself from the court and looks at it objectively that he realises the illusions under which he has lived. Both dukes, by being temporarily divorced from their normal lives, see life itself as being based on fantasy. As outsiders, however, they are the ones who are likened to dreamers. But the characters within their dreams, the characters they are observing, are real people who are themselves in a permanent state of illusion. Thus there is an ironic reversal of illusion and reality. Those describing themselves as 'dreamers' are experiencing a valid vision of life, whilst the supposedly 'awakened' members of society are living in a world of illusion. Both Malevole and Hercules have to attempt to waken the characters of illusion by bringing them into the outside world where the protagonists exist. This they both accomplish during the respective recognition scenes, although, ironically, as we have seen, Malevole through his success enters a new world of illusion. The dream-cycle begins again.

> We are such stuff
> As dreams are made on; and our little life
> Is rounded with a sleep.
>
> (*The Tempest*, IV. i. 156–8)

Prospero's words are acutely relevant. But if the characters within the plays oscillate between illusory and real worlds, what of the audience? For Marston was writing in a tradition which saw the plays themselves as dream situations. Lyly continually described his plays through the metaphor:

> There is no needles point so smal, which hath not his cõpasse nor haire so slender, which hath not his shadowe: nor sporte so simple, which hath not his showe. Whatsoeuer we presẽt, whether it be tedious (which we feare) or toyishe (which we doubt) sweete or sowre, absolute or imperfect, or whatsoeuer, in all humblenesse we all, & I on knee for all, entreate, that your Highnesse imagine your self to be in a deepe dreame, that staying the conclusiõ, in your rising your Maiestie vouchsafe but to saye, *And so you awakte*.
>
> (*Sapho and Phao*, Prologue at Court, 9–17)[2]

Similarly in the conclusion of the early play *The Taming of A Shrew* Slie tells the tapster:

> I have had
> The bravest dreame to night, that ever thou
> Hardest in all thy life. . . .
> I know now how to tame a shrew,

I dreamt upon it all this night till now,
And thou hast wakt me out of the best dreame
That ever I had in my life[3]

whilst Shakespeare concludes *A Midsummer Night's Dream* with:

If we shadows have offended,
Think but this, and all is mended,
That you have but slumb'red here
While these visions did appear.
And this weak and idle theme,
No more yielding but a dream,
Gentles, do not reprehend.
If you pardon, we will mend.
(*A Midsummer Night's Dream,* v. i. 412–19)

Two reasons for Lyly's comparison are given by Muriel Bradbrook, who tells us that as 'shadows' or 'dreams' the plays reflect the 'dalliance' of the royal court where they were performed, and that 'Lyly, like the nobles for whom he designed his offerings, was in search of reward.'[4] It is not, however, a far step from reflecting dalliance to satirising foolery, but Miss Bradbrook has given a deeper reason for artists' regarding plays in terms of a dream:

> Drama may evoke both superficial and deeply buried 'satellite selves', so that internal conflicts may be worked out to a more harmonious adjustment, a regrouping of impulses, a harmonising of partial systems. In this way, participation may correspond to the therapeutic function of a dream, and the final result will not by any means be just a fantasy gratification. The play dynamically frees and flexes relatively fixed and rigid images of the inner society. Therefore, if several roles attract identification, the plot becomes an exercise in the dynamics of adjustment, uniquely assisted by the fact that participation in drama is itself a social act. Conflicts can be projected more directly and more intensively. It cannot be expected that a given play will precisely correspond with the needs of any individual or at least, the odds are against it. Nevertheless, the result will not be fantasy gratification alone; it will be a return, through the release afforded by the exercise of fantasy in a context suggesting reality, to full reality.[5]

Dreams and plays are related. Both are helpful in releasing tensions within us, in acting as an outlet for repressive elements, whether the repression has been caused by civilisation or by its abuse. It is not fortuitous that, to discover the maladjustment of a mentally handicapped child, or that of its parents, psychiatrists study its behaviour in a play group. Through play the child comes to terms with the nature of its difficulties. What is drama but the playing of adults, the civilised two hours' licence given to the imagination? Peter Brook asserts, 'It is not by chance that in many languages the word for a play and to play is the same' (*The Empty Space*, p. 86). Hence drama, in releasing man's inhibitions, has an aim of aiding civilisation, even if the ideas it proposes are alien to that civilisation. Antonin Artaud agrees:

> Theatre will never be itself again, that is to say will never be able to form truly illusive means, unless it provides the audience with truthful distillations of dreams where its taste for crime, its erotic obsessions, its savageness, its fantasies, its utopian sense of life and objects, even its cannibalism, do not gush out on an illusory, make-believe, but on an inner level.[6]

This is exactly what some of Marston's plays do. The Thyestean banquet is placed before Piero in *Antonio's Revenge*, Antonio, Pandulpho and the rest being 'erotically obsessed' by their desire for revenge – a revenge which at first gains the sympathy or at least the full attention of the audience. Likewise, in the same play, Antonio's sensual and climactic killing of Julio is conducted with such frenzied fervency that the emotions of the audience are forced to take an active part in the scene. Their reaction is primarily emotional, leading either to a sensual identification of themselves with the murderer or to a horrific antagonism towards the act. By it they admit the viability of the deed in Antonio, in their neighbour, and ultimately in themselves. On the other hand Andrugio's 'utopian sense of life' in *Antonio and Mellida* draws a picture which the audience can appreciate as being of more value than the pomp of kings. Marston perhaps may be seen as one of those who gave his theatre the true life which Artaud sees now as having been lost. Artaud again:

> If theatre is as bloody and as inhuman as dreams the reason for this is that it perpetuates the metaphysical notions in some Fables in a present-day, tangible manner, whose atrocity and energy are enough to prove their origins and intentions in fundamental first principles rather than to reveal and unforgettably tie down the idea of continual conflict within us, where life is continually lacerated, where everything in creation rises up and attacks our condition as created beings.[7]

Thus image and spectacle naturally affect the subconscious, illustrating, by a direct means, the true realities of existence, the 'fundamental first principles'. It is in this respect that the ideas of Artaud and Bradbrook and the practice of Marston begin to resemble a surrealistic side of art, which, as Breton holds, aims 'to resolve the . . . contradictory conditions of dream and reality into an absolute reality, a super reality'.[8] This at first may seem very remote from Marston, but it becomes more relevant if in turning to the dramatist we draw a picture in words derived from one of his scenes.

In the centre of the picture is a man wearing a crown. In his hands he holds a skull filled with wine, which he offers to his lips as a toast to a number of other finely dressed yet foppish characters around him. Rushing through this crowd of finery and causing some excitement is a sailor. He appears to be shouting, and the shape of his head resembles somewhat that of the skull in the king's hands. To the left of the picture, just entering, is a feminine-looking page who appears to be starting to dance through the crowd. Above on a gallery is a woman running and shouting in a state of panic. To the right, a cold cynical man leans against a wall summing up the situation and singing sardonically. The king's face has an expression which is changing from delight to bewildered annoyance, whilst the whole scene is caricatured in the extreme and gives a total impression of speed and utter confusion. This fantastic picture is derived from the verbal imagery as well as the rapidity of the action in *Antonio and Mellida*, III. ii. 223–66. The episode creates an image in our minds of an over-all absurdity and confusion. Yet each aspect of the picture reveals a human actuality. There is pride, viciousness, cynicism, horror, laughter, panic, sycophancy, dance, relief – all mingled into one exaggerated scene which, in its seemingly illogical harmonisation of alien emotions and gross caricature, crystallises a composite vision of life. Here we are close to surrealist theatre.

Earlier in the same play we have experienced a similar scene (II. i) where Antonio, disguised as an Amazon, attends a court dance. Suddenly he falls to the ground, absurdly raving in Italian. The dancers' attitude is to be noted:

Antonio *Ohimè infelice misero, o lamentevol fato.*
[*Falls on the ground.*]
Alberto What means the lady fall upon the ground?
Rossaline Belike the falling sickness.
Antonio I cannot brook this sight; my thoughts grow wild;
Here lies a wretch on whom heaven never smil'd.
Rossaline [*To* Alberto.] What, servant, ne'er a word, and I here, man?
I would shoot some speech forth to strike the time

With pleasing touch of amorous compliment.
Say, sweet, what keeps thy mind? What think'st thou on?

Alberto Nothing.
Rossaline What's that nothing?
Alberto A woman's constancy.
Rossaline Good, why, would'st thou have us sluts, and never shift the vesture of our thoughts? Away for shame!
(*A & M*, II. i. 200–13)

The characters merely note the fact that a 'woman' has fallen to the ground. They look, comment and ignore. Their precious conversation continues and the 'girl' remains prostrate. The image for the audience is all that is needed to tell them about the society concerned. It is totally inhuman in that it is completely self-centred and self-oriented. Yet we do not forget the comic exaggeration of Antonio in his melodramatic antics and his absurd disguise. A complex satiric vision is being presented, so that the over-all image, rather than 'tying down' or 'revealing' a situation, agrees with what we might today call the Artaud thesis. It 'rises up and attacks our condition as human beings', and thus it laughs at the shadows that people regard as the reality of life. As Marston cried in an early satire, 'Oh hold my sides, that I may breake my spleene, / With laughter at the shadowes I haue seene.'[9]

In the other plays we find similar situations. *The Malcontent*, Act IV, scene ii, gives a visual and aural image of the total insularity of certain characters, but illustrates this through Marston's clever reversal of an Elizabethan attitude that saw 'Music . . . as reflecting the nature of the society in which it is produced' and 'harmonious music' as 'a microcosm of a well-ordered body politic'.[10] In *The Governor* Sir Thomas Elyot asserted,

> In euery daunse, of a moste auncient custome, there daunseth to gether a man and a woman, holding eche other by the hande or the arme, whiche betokeneth concorde. Nowe it behouethe the daunsers and also the beholders of them to knowe all qualities incident to a man, and also all qualities to a woman lyke wise appertaynynge. . . . These qualities, in this wise beinge knitte to gether, and signified in the personages of man and woman daunsinge, do expresse or sette out the figure of very nobilitie; whiche in the higher astate it is contained, the more excellent is the vertue in estimation.[11]

Dancing and music therefore could not only complement but signify to others the noble courtier. Castiglione held that music was 'meete to be practised in the presence of women, because those sights sweeten the mindes of the hearers, and make them more apt to bee pierced with the pleasantnesse of musicke, and also they quicken the spirits of the very doers'.[12] Earlier, however, Castiglione mocks the inordinate dancing of youth,[13] and it is from here that in his poetic satires, as Davenport suggests,[14] Marston took his cue to laugh at the ridiculous dancing postures of the fops:

> Who euer heard spruce skipping *Curio*
> Ere prate of ought, but of the whirle on toe.
> The turne aboue ground, *Robrus* sprauling kicks,
> *Fabius* caper, *Harries* tossing tricks?
> Did euer any eare, ere heare him speake
> Vnlesse his tongue of crosse-poynts did intreate?
> . . .
> His very soule, his intellectuall
> Is nothing but a mincing capreall.[15]

By the time Marston was writing *The Malcontent*, however, he saw that dance could be employed not merely as satire but also as a metaphor of the viciousness of Aurelia and Mendoza's court – the complete reversal therefore of the Elyot premise. In Act IV, scene ii, Aurelia enters from her bedchamber with Mendoza. The audience is aware that they both think that Pietro at this very time is being murdered. Aurelia calls for music: 'We will dance – music! – we will dance.' The dance chosen is Bianca's brawl, which in its description by the dancing-master shows itself to be as circumventing and intricate as the Machiavellianism that is ruling the court:

> 'tis but two singles on the left, two on the right, three doubles forward, a traverse of six round; to this twice, three singles side, galliard trick of twenty, coranto-space; a figure of eight, three singles broken down, come up, meet, two doubles, fall back, and then honour.
>
> (*The Malcontent*, IV. ii. 6–11)

Through all the complicated steps will eventually come 'honour' – a dancing term, but the irony is also evident. Following this description there is a great deal of stylised movement on stage, and this places the dance in a sinister grotesque relationship with the news of Pietro's death. Prepasso enters and asks for the duke; Aurelia demands 'Music!'. Equato appears and asks for the duke; Aurelia demands 'Music!'. Celso enters with the pointed remark, 'The duke is either quite invisible, or else is not', and is rebuked for his impertinence. A page enters and tells of where he last saw the duke, but

Aurelia again demands 'Music, sound high, as is our heart, sound high'. Malevole immediately enters with the disguised Pietro:

Malevole	The Duke – peace! [*The music stops.*] – the Duke is dead.
Aurelia	Music!
Malevole	Is't music?
Mendoza	Give proof.
Fernando	How?
Celso	Where?
Prepasso	When?
Malevole	Rest in peace, as the Duke does; quietly sit; for my own part, I beheld him but dead; that's all.

(IV. iii. 1–10)

The whole episode is peppered with abrupt entrances, pointed questions and ejaculations. The dance being played out is not the one to Aurelia's music but the grotesque and yet futile conduct of this depraved and debauched society, of which the Duchess's desired revels are merely another striking, almost surreal, metaphor.

Marston, however, never allows his surrealist images of tension, cruelty, horror and repulsion to affect merely the subconscious or the emotional. His plays have a dream-like quality which we are now inclined to associate with artists such as Artaud, but they also have the intellectual appeal of Brecht. The two designs are not, as is often thought, irreconcilable. On the contrary, Peter Brook holds that their union is the strength of the theatre:

> In all communication, illusions materialize and disappear. The Brecht theatre is a rich compound of images appealing for our belief. When Brecht spoke contemptuously of illusion, this was not what he was attacking. He meant the single sustained Picture, the statement that continued after its purpose had been served – like the painted tree.
>
> (*The Empty Space*, p. 88)

So often in Marston's plays we discover that as soon as an illusion is created it is destroyed. Andrugio, in *Antonio and Mellida* (IV. i), is Stoical in his defeat. He mocks greatness and decides that nature is his kingdom and his comfort. But, as we have seen, this image of the patient humble man is no sooner established than it is shattered by Lucio's reminding the duke of his former position. Andrugio's act fails and he raves like a madman.[16] This juxtaposing of images shocks the audience into an intellectual response, thereby preventing it on this occasion from any form of emotional involvement. The plays rely heavily on these reversal situations. In *Antonio's Revenge* Maria travels from Genoa to be reunited with her husband, only to find him dead, and Strotzo in the same play finds that support of Piero's lies and deceits brings not safety but death. In *Sophonisba* Massinissa's trust in the Carthaginian rulers is rewarded by treachery because of the sudden needs of a political solution, and in *The Insatiate Countess* Isabella's black mourning, which at first seems to be in sorrowful respect for her dead husband, is soon revealed to be only a manifestation of her lascivious and selfish character.

So as to shatter audience empathy, alienation techniques common to the twentieth-century stage – music, mime and commentary – are continually employed. The majority of his songs have been lost, but it is probable that their aim was to aid the intellectual progress of the drama by deliberately halting its narrative flow, or providing a vivid contrast to or commentary on the action on stage. Balurdo's 'My mistress' eye doth oil my joints' succeeds Antonio's murder of Julio. In doing so it refocuses our attention from the horror of the death to the folly of sexual perversion at court:

> My mistress' eye doth oil my joints
> And makes my fingers nimble;
> O love, come on, untruss your points –
>
> *My fiddlestick wants rosin.*
>
> My lady's dugs are all so smooth
> That no flesh must them handle;
> Her eyes do shine, for to say sooth,
> Like a new-snuffed candle.
>
> (*AR*, III. ii. 30–7)

The 'fiddlestick' innuendo is crude in its demand for laughter, but nevertheless our attention has been switched by the comic intrusion. In similar fashion Franceschina's *'Cantat Gallice'* in *The Dutch Courtesan* (II. ii. 54–60) is in contrast both to her anger preceding Freevill's entrance and Malheureux's present melancholia, although the song takes the opportunity, despite the 'frolic', to 'still complain me do her wrong'. Another example is found in *The Malcontent*, Act II, scene v. Here, whilst a song is being sung, Ferneze flies from Aurelia's bedchamber only to be met by Mendoza's sword. The music is cut short by the tumult, but the contrast between the luxuriousness of the bedchamber probably implied by the song, and the reality of Ferneze's 'death' would have been vivid.[17] The preceding scene is also illustrative of further subtle uses of contrast. Whilst Ferneze is off stage enjoying Aurelia's bed, the audience is aware that he is also endangering his life. Maquerelle, in the meantime, enters with Emilia and Bianca. Her conversation with the two girls concerns the ingredients and sexual properties of a love potion. The old bawd is encouraging them in the arts of lust, whilst off stage we are aware that it is lust which is putting Ferneze in a perilous situation. The contrast between Maquerelle's instruction, together with its enthusiastic acceptance by the girls, and the realities that are about to occur, provides yet another picture of the futility of this lascivious court.

Contrast is evident also in the frequent use of the dumb show. In *Antonio and Mellida*, for example, occur the stage directions

> *The cornets sound a sennet. Enter above,* Mellida Rossaline *and* Flavia. *Enter below* Galeatzo *with attendants;* Piero [*enters,*] *meeteth him, embraceth; at which the cornets sound a flourish.* Piero *and* Galeatzo *exeunt. The rest stand still.*
>
> Mellida What prince was that passed through my father's guard?
> Flavia 'Twas Galeatzo, the young Florentine.
>
> (I. i. 99–100)

The girls continue by criticising the figure of Galeatzo and praising the memory of Antonio. Following this comes another dumb show – with the second suitor, Matzagente – and a similar conversation from the girls. The dumb show, as Dieter Mehl tells us, is consequently being contrasted with the objective comments of the onlookers:

> In both scenes only characters from the play itself take part. The effectiveness of the silent scene lies chiefly in the pointed gestures and the musical accompaniment; it seems likely that the pompous atmosphere of the court was indicated by the presence of servants and the whole style of acting. Piero's triumph . . . and his intention of marrying Mellida off to some powerful prince are impressively portrayed, and at the same time they are shown in a particular light because of the dramatic method employed. The use of silent action alone for such an incident could, especially if accompanied by exaggerated gestures, give the whole scene an unnatural and slightly comic character. That this was the author's intention is emphasised by the simultaneous conversation in the gallery which reveals Mellida's opinion of her father's schemes quite clearly. The spectator thus sees the scene through Mellida's

eyes because she makes her scornful remarks about the two suitors as the events on the stage are explained to her. . . . The silent scene throws a somewhat sarcastic light upon life at the court and on the two suitors. Mellida's commentary heightens this effect and reveals her own attitude to the events.[18]

Commentary itself acts as a similar alienating agent. We have seen it operative with Feliche, Malevole and Mendoza, but sometimes it is merely a line, rather than a speech, that prevents total empathy. During the scene in which the revengers murder Piero in *Antonio's Revenge*, they create, as we have seen, an almost ecstatic sensual rhythm of violence as they approach the deed, but the ridiculous presence of Balurdo prevents the audience from losing itself totally in their action. His three lines,

> Down to the dungeon with him; I'll dungeon with him; I'll fool you! Sir Jeffery will be Sir Jeffery. I'll tickle you!
>
> (*AR*, v. iii. 69–70)

> Thou most retort and obtuse rascal!
>
> (*AR*, v. iii. 99)

are just enough to alienate the audience, reminding it that it is in a dream situation. Similarly, a possible explanation for the painter's introduction in *Antonio and Mellida*, Act v, scene i, is in terms of alienation – the author telling us something about himself and the composition of the work:

> Balurdo And are these the workmanship of your hands?
> Painter I did limn them.
> Balurdo 'Limn them'? a good word, 'limn them.' Whose picture is this? [*Reads.*] *'Anno Domini* 1599.' Believe me, master Anno Domini was of a good settled age when you limn'd him; 1599 years old! Let's see the other. [*Reads.*] *'Aetatis suae 24.'* By'r Lady, he is somewhat younger. Belike master *Aetatis suae* was *Anno Domini's* son.
>
> (*A & M*, v. i. 3–11)[19]

The alienation scene prepares us for the play's conclusion by allowing time for us to recollect our thoughts before we are plunged into the complexities of Andrugio and Antonio's 'deaths'. Although these devices are sometimes crude in exposition, Marston illustrates a mastery in fusing such alienation techniques with the validity of dream involvement. In our role as spectators we watch Marston's plays throughout with a mixed response. We can sympathise with the characters, we can become involved with the action and we can objectively criticise both characters and action; but in having such a mixed response we show an over-all appreciation of Marston's art. He illustrates his ability to combine the essentials of the theatre, appealing to our emotions, our subconscious, our intellect and our reason – often all at the same time and within the one satiric genre. The primary example of this expertise in action is during that almost surrealist scene in *Antonio and Mellida* (III. ii. 223–62). Our intellect appreciates the word images of Piero in describing how he will drink from Antonio's skull; our emotions are with the young prince as he attempts to escape; our subconscious takes in the vast image of contradictory emotions presented on stage; and our reason (alerted by Feliche's alienating device of the song) evaluates all that has occurred. This is true theatre in illustrating the harmonious combination of so many varying attitudes towards the art. It shows how Marston can claim his art to be 'seriously fantastical'[20] – a phrase which perhaps defines the nature of his satiric dreams.

8
Productions and Adaptations

The way in which Marston creates his composite dramatic images testifies to his technical ability as a playwright. It is not surprising, therefore, that the texts show a lively concern for stage directions, for the play in production. Dieter Mehl writes,

> In reading his plays one feels that the writer had a practical experience of the theatre and knew how to make use of it. In Marston's plays the rhetorical element, though very strong, only contributes to the dramatic movement of the incidents on the stage. At the same time stage directions are used much more frequently and consciously than in the work of many other dramatists to make the spoken word more effective and expressive.[1]

Thus *Sophonisba* for example, opens with a striking display:

> *Cornets sound a march.*
> *Enter at one dore the* Prologue*: too Pages with torches:* Asdrubal *and* Jugurth *too Pages with lights:* Massinissa *leading* Sophonisba*:* Zanthia *bearing* Sophonisbas *traine* Arcathia *and* Nicea*:* Hano *and* Bytheas. *At the other dore too Pages with targets and Javelines, too Pages with lights,* Syphax *armd from top to toe,* Vangue *followes.*
> *These thus entred, stand still, whilst the* Prologue *resting betweene both troups speakes.*
> The Sceane is *Lybia*, and the subject thus.
> Whilst *Carthage* stoode. . . .
>
> (*Sophonisba*, p. 7)

Production was plainly in the dramatist's mind here. Visual, oral and aural elements are employed. There is a symmetry demanding attention for the majesty of what is to follow, a dramatic formality designed to stir audience feelings from the beginning. Many modern comparisons could be made, but an obvious one would be with

Trevor Nunn's opening of *Julius Caesar* in Stratford 1972. The army marched on, flags and banners flew, drums rolled and Caesar stood head erect acknowledging the loud adulation of his troops. However good or bad the performance, the opening was theatrical. So too with the stage directions in the Marston text. In play after play a theatrical awareness of a director–writer is shown. Often it is manifested through the insistence on symmetry:

> *Enter* Brabant Junior *at one doore,* Ned Planet *at the other.*
> (*Jack Drum*, p. 189)

> *Enter two Pages, the one laughing, the other crying.*
> (*Jack Drum*, p. 191)

> *Enter* Plenty *in Majesty, upon a Throne, heapes of gold,* Plutus, Ceres; *and* Bachus *doing homage.*
> (*Histriomastix*, p. 256)[2]

> *Enter* Pride, Vaine-glory, Hypocrisie, *and* Contempt: Pride *casts a mist, wherein* Mavortius *and his company vanish off the Stage, and* Pride *and her attendants remaine.*
> (*Histriomastix*, p. 268)

> *The vilest out-of-tune music being heard, enter* Bilioso *and* Prepasso.
>
> Bil. [*Shouts to the upper level of the stage.*] . . .
>
> *Enter one with a perfume.*
> (*The Malcontent*, I. i.)

> *Enter the* Duke Pietro, Ferrardo,Count Equato, Count Celso *before, and* Guerrino
> (*The Malcontent*, I. ii.)

> *The cornets sound a sennet. Enter* Feliche *and* Alberto, Castilio *and* Forobosco, *a page carrying a shield,* Piero *in armor,* Catzo *and* Dildo *and* Balurdo. *All these (saving* Piero*) armed with petronels. Being enter'd, they make a stand in divided files.*
> (*Antonio and Mellida,* I. i.)

There is a certain concentration on production detail in these examples. Celso enters just in front of Pietro and the others. Piero's authority is emphasised by the sound of the sennet, by his armour and by the fact that all but he carry the petronels. Symmetry is demanded in that they stand in 'divided files'. The 'vilest out-of-tune music' in its peculiarity shocks the audience to attention.

Brabant Junior and Ned Planet simultaneously arrive on stage but at different entrances. Backs to their respective doors, they begin their dialogues. These might seem all minor points, but in production it is such attention to visual detail and precision that gains the required theatrical effect and helps to make a good play into a success.

We have already seen Marston's fondness for tableau effects, whether surreal or not. Many of the plays seem to be constructed of short sharp scenes building up a stylised historical or narrative effect in a manner similar to a medieval tapestry. Visual impact often is stressed at the expense of characterisation, and the whole is directed away from normality by the juvenile nature of the actors. The children did not have to be precocious to gain this effect, although at times, especially in the earlier plays, precocity was deliberately employed by the dramatist. In *Sophonisba* the child actors are given not a grotesque or satiric role, but a heavily stylised one which lends an added dimension to the gravity of the plot, in the manner of the emblematic figures of, for example, the Bayeux tapestry. A problem in production, however, must have occurred if the plays were to be performed by the adult companies.[3] As far as it is known, during Marston's theatrical career this transference occurred only with *The Malcontent*:

Sly	I would know how you came by this play.
Condell	Faith, sir, the book was lost; and because 'twas pity so good a play should be lost, we found it, and play it.
Sly	I wonder you would play it, another company having interest in it.
Condell	Why not Malevole in folio with us, as Jeronimo in decimo-sexto with them? They taught us a name for our play: we call it *One for another*.
Sly	What are your additions?
Burbage	Sooth, not greatly needful; only as your sallet to your great feast, to entertain a little more time, and to abridge the not-received custom of music in our theatre.

(*The Malcontent*, Induction, 72–84)

There are a number of important points here. The first is related not so much to the way in which the King's Men acquired the play, as to the irony that they wanted to produce the work of a man and company that had been so satirical about them. It is no longer enough for Rosencrantz to complain of the berattling of the common stages.[4] The public companies are answering the Paul's and Blackfriars by, we might say, joining them. The best ways to repulse an attack are by attacking yourself or by allying yourself with your antagonists. It seems that Marston had no objection to the King's

Men producing one of his satirical comedies, since he provided at least some of the additions and probably saw the revised version through the press.[5] The second point of interest concerns the way in which the tenor of the play must have been altered by the transference from the boys to the adults. It is a difficult problem, since we cannot be certain of stage conditions and performance techniques at the respective theatres. But a tentative answer may stem from Burbage's comment that alterations have been made 'to entertain a little more time, and to abridge the not-received custom of music in our theatre'. Professor Hunter has demonstrated that extra scenes and speeches have increased the line content of the play, thus 'raising [it] to something more like the average length of Globe plays';[6] and, referring to a suggestion by W. J. Lawrence, has noted that two meanings can be ascribed to the music reference: 'either the overture and/or interludes were dispensed with, or else certain integral musical features of the play itself were omitted'.[7] The latter does not seem to be so, since, textually, there is only one omission of a song from the quarto of the Globe's play in comparison with the quartos of the Blackfriars.[8] It seems, therefore, that, if the musical content was reduced, it would probably have been in the overture and the interludes between the acts. There is no way in which we can discover the exact nature of this music. If, however, it was employed similarly to the examples of musical effects and songs that we find in the main body of the text, then certain hypotheses deserve attention. Christian Kiefer has illustrated how throughout the play music serves the purpose of being 'a symptom of hypocrisy and deception'.[9] As seen elsewhere,[10] and noted by Kiefer, music is continually being employed in incongruous situations. Aurelia's desire for music at the time of the announcement of Pietro's death, and the discordant notes that open the play are the principal examples. The latter sets the tone of disharmony that is to prevail throughout, but its effect would have been increased if in the Blackfriars production it had followed, almost in imitation, a musical overture. The harmony entertaining the audience before the performance began would have implicitly exacerbated the effect of Malevole's opening cacophony.[11] In the Globe production such a musical contrast would not have taken place if the overture and interludes were omitted. It is important to note that, of the augmentations and additions in the Globe production, four occur in places in which there may formerly have been such a musical interlude. The first of these is Webster's Induction – a possible replacement for the overture – which not only talks of the history of the play, but also, as we have seen, of its dramatic and satiric nature. The second is the final scene of Act I, in which Malevole and Passarello entertain the audience in a jest-book fashion. Interestingly enough, the episode begins with Malevole asking Passarello, the only character who does not appear in the Blackfriars production, 'Canst sing, fool?' (I. viii. 1). Why talk of music at this moment? There has been no textual incentive to do so. Perhaps it is because the author is writing a new scene at the end of the first act as a replacement for the musical interlude which at the Blackfriars probably occurred between Acts I and II. Obviously this can only be speculation, but it is interesting that most of the first scene of Act III and the whole of the first scene of Act V are similarly additions to the Blackfriars performance, although there is no addition between Acts III and IV. It seems possible, therefore, that the Induction and the three other additions cited above (I. viii; III. i. 34–150; V. i. 1–55) may be replacements for 'the not-received custom of music in our theatre' – that is, for the overture and the interludes.

These, however, are not the only additions/augmentations made for the Globe performance. The others are no less significant in our evaluation of the tenor of the play in production. Without exception, each of the scenes peculiar to the Globe involves either Malevole or the newly created character Passarello, and, on occasions, both. In discussing these alterations our attention should be turned to the theories of Foakes and Caputi concerning the nature of the boy actors adding the element of the grotesque through the mimicry of the adult world. Little boys or even young adolescents ridiculing through imitation the Machiavellian policies and pride of courts, and the sexual ingenuity of whores and bawds, helped to create the nightmarish surrealist quality of the plays that has been discussed earlier. This element would have been subtracted from the performance at the Globe and consequently the play would have been in danger of being weakened in its effectiveness. The augmentation, therefore, besides (and at times including) the replacement for the music, may be seen as complementary in creating a tonality to those elements lost through transition. Thus the addition at I. iii. 108–49 has Malevole showing his grotesque 'hideous imagination' by describing the logical consequences of Mendoza and Aurelia's incestuous relationship. Similarly, lines 155–72 of the same scene illustrate Malevole's malcontented mind and grotesque desire:

> Lean thoughtfulness, a sallow meditation,
> Suck thy veins dry, distemperance rob thy sleep!
> (156–7)

In several additions (I. iv. 43–89; II. iii. 23–37; V. iii. 66–97) the malcontent exposes the repulsive sycophancy of Bilioso, who in the first of them even insinuates that he will prostitute his wife for personal gain and advantage: 'I'll make thee acquainted with my young wife too. What! I keep her not at court for nothing. 'Tis grown to supper-time; come to my table: that, anything I have, stands open to thee' (I. iv. 71–4).

Of the remaining fifth-act interpolations, one (V. iv. 19–34) sustains Malevole's malcontented role, while the other (V. vi. 137–58) helps to bring about the moral contrast already noted, between pretentious, patronising Altofront and the 'dead' Malevole.[12] The other interpolations all include the clown, Passarello, who provides that peculiar detached yet pertinent wit found so often in the jest-book roles played by Elizabethan comedians such as Robert Armin:

Malevole You are in good case since you came to court, fool. What, guarded, guarded!
Passarello Yes, faith, even as footmen and bawds wear velvet, not for an ornament of honour, but for a badge of drudgery; for, now the Duke is discontented, I am fain to fool him asleep every night.
Malevole What are his griefs?
Passarello He hath sore eyes.
Malevole I never observed so much.
Passarello Horrible sore eyes; and so hath every cuckold, for the roots of the horns spring in the eyeballs, and that's the reason the horn of a cuckold is as tender as his eye, or as that growing in the woman's forehead twelve years since, that could not endure to be touched. The Duke hangs down his head like a columbine.

(I. viii. 7–21)

The cuckoldry explanation is striking in its oddity and yet relevant. Jealousy, as Leontes shows, can come with a look; and suspicion and accusation, as Edward II proves, can force a woman to cuckold her husband. In its distance and yet relevance to the main action, the fool's role in the revised version of *The Malcontent* shares similar qualities with the grotesque distance that the boys naturally had from their parts throughout the play:

Malevole Give me the bowl. I drink the health to Altofront, our deposed Duke. [*Drinks*.]
Passarello I'll take it so. [*Takes back bowl, and drinks*.] Now I'll begin a health of Madam Maquerelle. [*Drinks*.]
Malevole Pooh! I will not pledge her.
Passarello Why, I pledged your Lord.
Malevole I care not.
Passarello Not pledge Madam Maquerelle! why, then, will I spew up your lord again with this fool's finger.

Malevole Hold; I'll take it. [*Takes bowl, and drinks.*]
Maquerelle [*To* Malevole.] Now thou hast drunk my health.
Fool, I am friends with thee.
Passarello Art? art?
When Griffon saw the reconcilèd quean
Offering about his neck her arms to cast,
He threw off sword and heart's malignant stream,
And lovely her below the loins embraced. –
Adieu, Madam Maquerelle.
(v. ii. 22–39)

Visually as well as aurally there is a repulsiveness here as Passarello bends his knees, thrusts out his head and prepares to push his fingers into his throat. His purpose is to maintain the detachment of grotesque humour, the bitterness to which Webster had already referred in the Induction. Even Bilioso sees this quality in the clown:

Passarello Your fool will stand for your lady most willingly and most uprightly.
Bilioso I'll salute her in Latin.
Passarello O, your fool can understand no Latin.
Bilioso Ay, but your lady can.
Passarello Why, then, if your lady take down your fool, your fool will stand no longer for your lady.
Bilioso A pestilent fool! . . .
Didst thou see Madam Florio to-day?
Passarello Yes, I found her repairing her face today; the red upon the white showed as if her cheeks should have been served in for two dishes of barberries in a stewed broth, and the flesh to them a woodcock.
Bilioso A bitter fool!
(III. i. 118–25, 136–41)

The interpolations in the Globe performance were plainly handled with skill, maintaining those grotesque qualities of satiric tragedy which had made the play a success at the Blackfriars. Consequently those elements which the play necessarily was in danger of losing by its transference from the one theatre to the other – certainly the air of detachment that the boy actors added to the play, and possibly the complementary nature of the interlude music with the preceding and succeeding acts – were fully compensated for in the creation of the bitter grotesque clown, the extension of Malevole's hideous imagination and the further exaggeration of Bilioso's repulsive sycophancy.

Transference from the original theatre to others has not always had such an easy history in the life of Marston's other plays. Marston retired from the theatre in about 1608, although his departure did not mean the immediate withdrawal of his plays from the repertoire. *The Insatiate Countess,* if acted at the Whitefriars as the title pages of the quartos assure us, must have been performed after 1607, 'since that is the earliest possible year for the activation of that theatre'.[13] *The Dutch Courtesan* was performed at least twice in 1613[14] and *The Malcontent* was being performed in 1635.[15] During the closure of the theatres under the Puritans, the Cocledemoy–Mulligrub plot of *The Dutch Courtesan* was used as a droll entitled *The Cheater Cheated.*[16] As early, in fact, as February 1613, *The Dutch Courtesan* had been retitled *Cockle de Moye*, thus showing the popularity of the sub-plot,[17] but the first major adaptation of the complete play was published in 1680 under the title *The Revenge; or A Match in Newgate.*[18] This adaptation and those by Christopher Bullock in 1715, *A Woman's Revenge; or A Match in Newgate*, and a ballad opera *Love and Revenge; or The Vintner Outwitted* in 1729 are interesting in the way that, in their desire to 'improve' the play according to Restoration and eighteenth-century tastes, they become involved in all the inherent moral and narrative complexities and problems which, as we saw earlier, Marston himself had failed to conquer completely. The result is an increasing confusion concerning the morality and characterisation in the drama.

The 1680 production, *The Revenge*, at the Duke's Theatre is the principal example of this. From the alterations made to the original play it is plain that the adapter was aware that there were inherent problems but lost as to their essential nature or, at least, as to how they could be satisfactorily resolved. The result is a tinkering with the text that exacerbates the romance–reality conflict to produce a sentimental melodrama largely divorced from the complex thematic concerns of its predecessor.

All the characters' names are changed, not without significance. Thus instead of unhappy Malheureux the adapter produces Mr Friendly, and for Freevill we find the alteration Wellman. Similarly, Cocledemoy becomes Trickwell; Franceschina, Corina; Crispinella, Diana; Tysefew, Sir John Empty; and Beatrice, Marinda. More important, the allegorical significance in theme is correspondingly altered. Ironically enough, by creating Friendly the author was reverting to an original conception in the plot source where the friendship motif between the two men is 'their first loyalty',[19] but even here the adapter becomes confused, since he is not sure which thematic considerations he should emphasise. Thus he resorts to the exigency of tidying up the plot first and fitting in thematic concerns where they seem to be important. He was obviously not satisfied with the lack of symmetry in Marston's design. There are two principal 'virtuous' male characters and two principal virtuous female characters in *The Dutch Courtesan*, but, whereas Freevill marries Beatrice, there is no corresponding attachment between Malheureux and Crispinella. The romantic answer is to begin the play by portraying Friendly in love with Diana and by reworking the plot so that in the conclusion they will marry. This 'tidying up' attempts to bring about two 'improvements'. First, it means that in the end the narrative will be neatly but sentimentally resolved. Secondly, it provides an ingenious reason why the Malheureux figure has an attachment with the whore. Diana at first rebuffs Friendly's professions of love because he is not a full man. In her opinion, which has understandably evolved from the Montaigne influence in Marston, a chaste man has no business in asking for her hand: 'I'm for no such dull Ingredience in a Lover: I love a man that knows the way to a womans bed without instructions' (*The Revenge*, p. 12). Thus she will not consider Friendly for a husband until he has had an affair: 'Let him but bring it under the hand of any woman who has been kinde to him, and I'll believe him fit to be belov'd by me; till then, I am obdurate' (p. 12). He is therefore given approval to approach Corina, and by implication Wellman's previous immorality is similarly excused. Montaigne's philosophy is exonerated by the symmetry of the plot design and awkward questions necessarily raised by the Marston story are swept aside.

There is, however, still the question of the whore. The moral problems raised in Marston's play by the 'justice' shown to Franceschina in the conclusion are similarly dismissed by the symmetrical preoccupation of the Restoration dramatist. Corina too is allowed to marry at the end, since the Tysefew character, Sir John Empty, cannot be married off to Diana. Thus Empty is enchanted by Corina's looks and she is persuaded by Wellman to accept him, the gallant in the process excusing his own misconduct:

Wellman — By Heaven, *Corina*, it was not want of Love, my Fortune did depend upon my Marriage, but when I saw the Woman destin'd for me, I must confess I felt new flames possess me, without extinguishing the old, and I resolv'd to love her virtuously, and hold an honest Friendship still with thee – to raise thee up above the Worlds contempt, the fickle favours of unconstant man, and love thee as my Sister.

Corina — What pow'rful Charms dwell in thy tender language! thou melt'st my rage with every softening look and lead'st me a tame Captive to thy will; . . . I am still all thine, dispose me as thou pleasest.

(*The Revenge*, pp. 61–2)

The obvious attempt to reconcile the moral problem here only leads to false sentimentality and a probable worsening of the theme-plot conflict, by introducing the concepts of Fortune and the trivial statement of loving the whore as a sister. Although attempting through the convenience of Empty to resolve the Franceschina problem, the adapter throughout the play shows a complete lack of understanding about the nature of her original. Marston's theatrical restraint, even in his largely abortive attempt to deal with the problem, is ignored and even worked against. Thus the Dutch accent, which as we have seen is dramatically so important, is dismissed, as are the psychological subtleties in the Marston creation. The adapter seems to imagine, for example, that we need an excuse to find sympathy for the whore and so he exaggerates that small episode in *The Dutch Courtesan* (IV. iii. 1–16) in which Cocledemoy crudely taunts Franceschina with sexual innuendo. In *The Revenge* these sixteen lines are turned into an attempted rape scene, in which Corina's virtue is saved only by the intervention of Wellman, and it is only Corina's honest entreaty that prevents Wellman from killing Trickwell.

Corina Hold, do not kill the Raskal; 'tis enough you've saved me from his mischiefs: pray let him go.
Wellman 'Tis pitie, but I will obey. Take that, and that, that, ye Mungrel Cur; Dogs shou'd be us'd so [*Kicks him out.*] Death! what a wretched thing's a Whore, that every Raskal dares approach with Love! [*Aside.*]
(p. 41)

Similarly, *The Dutch Courtesan*, Act II, scene ii, in which Freevill refuses to give Franceschina the ring he had from Beatrice, is extended for a banal theatrical effect. Vacuous sentimentality is introduced early in this episode, since Marinda has given the ring an added value. It belonged to her dead brother: 'Here, wear this little Ring; a dying Brother gave it, and bad me never part with it but to him that Love had made my Husband' (*The Revenge*, p. 12). When the gallant refuses to give it to Corina, the whore, as in Marston, loses her temper. But in the Restoration play she rages to such an extent that quite farcically she takes a gun with which she has already threatened the bawd, and fires it at Wellman. It fails to work correctly.

Corina Farewel. And dost thou think I'll part with thee thus tamely! Faithless unthinking fool, by Heaven, no other woman shall possess thee; the perjur'd heart you gave, thus I demand:

Takes a Pistol out of her pocket, fires it at his breast; it onely flashes in the pan: Friendly *runs to her; she throws it away.*

> Oh damn this treacherous instrument fake as the heart 'twas aim'd at: But since, like Coward States, I wanted courage to attack the Foe, I'll turn my Fury into civil Broyls, and hurl all to confusion here within.

Offers to stab her self; Friendly *runs to her, prevents her, and she seems fainted a little while in his arms.*

(p. 19)

The adapter is again taking the simplest way out of the problems that beset the Marston play. He opts for sentimental and melodramatic theatrical effects which ignore rather than solve the difficulties. Thus one of the reasons why Friendly is at first rebuked by the dissembling whore is that he is a traitor to his friendship with Wellman (p. 10). Even in the sub-plot Trickwell is given a just cause for his treatment of the Mulligrub character, Mr Dashit.[20] Furthermore, although vestiges and lines of Montaigne remain, the morality questions become relevant only in their appropriateness to the dictates of the new symmetry, which in itself reduces the dramatic concept of the original. In attempting to improve the work the adapter consequently succeeded only in reducing its intellectual appeal.

From *The Revenge* the degeneration continued. In 1715 Christopher Bullock produced at the New Theatre, Lincoln's Inn Fields, *A Woman's Revenge*, with himself as Vizard, 'a notorious Cheat'; Mr Bullock Snr as Mr Thinkwell, the father of Celia (Beatrice); and Mr H. Bullock as a fiddler! The play is an adaptation of *The Revenge*, but this time the whore, Corinna, is finally paid off by the gallant, Freeman, so long as she 'can forgoe' her 'former Course of Living'.[21] By 1729, due to the vogue of ballad opera following *The Beggar's Opera* of 1728, Bullock had turned the play into a musical. The thematic decline was complete, since Malheureux, the puritanical man of snow, had become Rovewell, and free-living Freevill, Trueman. The main plot, now bankrupt of interest, was omitted from the later eighteenth-century versions of the play; in such pieces as *Trick for Trick* (1739) and *The Vintner Trick'd* (1746), only the farce remained.[22]

The next significant date in the history of Marston productions is in the nineteenth century, although in 1775, at the Theatre Royal, Drury Lane, Mrs Lennox did present under the title *Old City Manners*, a version of Jonson, Chapman and Marston's *Eastward Hoe*. But it is a production in 1850 that must attract our attention. On 5 July 1850 a notice appeared in *The Times* to the effect that the Royal

Olympic Theatre was to be let. On Friday 26 July a further notice appeared:

> OLYMPIC THEATRE – Mr. GEO. BOLTON begs respectfully to inform the public that he has taken the above theatre for six nights commencing Monday next, with the purpose of reviving THE MALCONTENT (written by John Marston 250 years ago) – a play which may vie with many a production of Shakespeare. To be followed by a Dramatic Squib, introducing Mde Louise, Rosina Wright, and the most powerful ballet company in London. With other Entertainments. Boxes, 2s. 6d.; pit, 1s. gallery, 6d.

The production caused 'some sensation in Wych-street' (*The Times*, 30 July 1850), not only amongst the audience but also with the critics. The reviewers in the main were decided that it was a poor performance, but in detail their accounts are quite varied. *The Spectator* (3 August) saw Bolton's initiative as a 'theatrical nullity', and continued, 'when it is evident that Dodsley has been opened at haphazard, and when the company is such that mediocrity is only relieved by utter badness, a revival of the sort is below criticism'. Most agreed that the company was mediocre or even worse, G. H. Lewes in *The Leader* (3 August) calling it 'the most incompetent company in London' and *The Weekly Dispatch* (4 August) holding that the performance was 'marred by the inefficiency of the *corps dramatique*'. *The Illustrated London News* (3 August), however, thought 'the piece was cleverly acted', and *The Observer* (4 August), although 'disapproving of the production', felt that 'it must be added . . . that it was carefully got up and respectably acted'. This reviewer continues by telling us that the 'performers, excepting Mrs Brougham, were all strangers to the town'. *The Weekly Dispatch* names three of the company whose performances were the exception to the rule of inefficiency:

> For, if we except Mr. James Johnstone, as *Altofronto* (and even he out-Herods Herod, and rants more than even such a ranting character requires), Mr. W. Atwood, as *Passarello*, and Mrs. Griffiths, as *Maguerelle* [sic], the less we say about the other actors, will, perhaps be the better, both for their peace of mind, and our reputation as good-natured critics.

For its part, *Lloyd's Weekly Newspaper* (4 August) noted that 'Mr. H. Lee acted creditably, and Mrs. Brougham and Miss Murray did all that could be done for two characters for which the author had done nothing', but it was in general agreement that the acting was 'of a very mediocre description, most of the characters being inefficiently sustained'. The reviewer, however, also tells us a little more about Johnstone's actual performance:

> Mr. Johnstone . . . is a most respectable actor; but Malevole is a part in which he is much overweighted. The scene in which he describes himself, and the manner in which he delivered that description, was the best part of Mr. Johnstone's performance. . . . Mr. Johnstone delivered this speech ['I cannot sleep . . .'–III. ii.] with good emphasis and sound discretion. He outraged some of the scenes by rant and melodramatic action.

The Observer adds that, with Mr Johnstone, 'Mr. H. Lee, Mr. Simpson . . . and Mr. Marshall seem to be men of talent, which deserves to be better employed.' Thus, although most seem to be agreed that the company was poor, they all make different exceptions and so make nearly all the actors talented. Such is the nature of theatre reviews.

The content of the play itself also troubled the critics. *The Weekly Dispatch* praises the principle of reviving plays by 'Shakespeare and the elder dramatists', but continues, 'managers, like mortals, must be content often to deserve success, without commanding it'. Mr Bolton, it seems, had chosen the wrong drama to revive. The reason for this was given by *The Observer*: '[Marston] has the faults of his greater contemporaries, not redeemed by their beauties'; though the critic continues,

> Not that he was destitute of dramatic talent. He had a knowledge of human nature, was a shrewd satirist of the follies and vices of his time, and his plays are full of pregnant sayings; but they are also polluted by coarse and filthy ribaldry; and his serious passages indicate neither the tenderness, passion, imagination, nor splendour of poetical diction, for which the writers of that age were distinguished.

Clearly it was the attack by Marston's style on their Victorian sensibility that concerned the critics most. In the opinion of *The Morning Post* (30 July),

> The plays of John Marston have the besetting sins of his age – profanity and obscenity. The latter vice is so closely interwoven with his plots that any attempt to cleanse them from their impurities is a task as futile as was the labour of Sisyphus.

George Bolton, however, had undertaken the labour by producing an adaptation of the play, praised by *Lloyds*:

> In the version under notice, we have no interpolations of the adapter; he has wisely confined himself to a judicious curtailment, and to the omission of the many objectionable passages contained in the original.

But the editing did not help to make it acceptable to *The Observer*:

> In short, the play is an exhibition of various forms of vice; there is only one person sufficiently virtuous to excite any interest, and she occupies a subordinate part in the plot.

Unbelievably, 'the audience, which was numerous, seemed well pleased' (*Illustrated London News*), so that the play 'was applauded at termination, and Mr. Bolton called before the curtain' (*Morning Post*). But, as *The Observer* ruefully notes,

> When the curtain fell there was very loud but by no means general applause, with audible sounds of disapprobation. Every piece, good or bad, is now-a-days applauded more or less; but it is impossible that such a piece as this could be satisfactory to the bulk of an English audience.

However, *The News of the World* critic (4 August), dismissing the 'dry and tedious affair', tells us that the production 'met with faint applause', and the majority of papers seemed to agree with *The Times* that, 'as a dramatic curiosity', the play 'may draw for the remainder of the six nights, but as for its becoming a piece of the *repertoire*, it is out of the question'. *The Morning Post* observed, 'its continuance will doubtless depend upon the patronage awarded by the public'. Yet perhaps it was the public that proved to be the best critics, since they ensured an extension of the 'run' from the proposed six to eighteen nights. The final word on the whole affair should be left to the brave critic of *The London Mercantile Journal* (6 August):

> Mr. George Bolton . . . is eminently a theatrical *student*, and has found heaps of almost forgotten treasures in the course of his researches. Almost every one has heard of 'rare Ben Johnson' [sic] but not one playgoer in a hundred has ever seen one of his noble dreams acted: and the same may be said of a whole galaxy of [Elizabethan–Jacobean] dramatists. . . . Marston was one of these pithy geniuses, and Mr. Bolton has tried the experiment of reviving his tragicomedy of the *Malcontent*. No small section of the modern race of critics do not relish it, because their taste has become vitiated by melo drama; but we are honest enough to dare

to be old-fashioned, and pronounce the experiment a boon to dramatic literature.

It may be that this reviewer was less 'old-fashioned' than far-sighted.

The major English productions of Marston this century began in 1954 with Joan Littlewood's production of *The Dutch Courtesan* at the Theatre Workshop, Stratford East. Miss Littlewood produced the play on a twin-level set designed by Peter Snow. Avis Bunnage played Franceschina 'as a real woman and not a stage slut' and George Cooper created a Cocledemoy who was 'a joy'.[23] But, as in the nineteenth century, the reviewers tended to have some disagreements – *The Times* (24 February 1954) seeing it as an 'imaginative and often beautiful production', while *The Daily Telegraph* (24 February) declared it to be 'an uneven and unexciting work eminently worthy of another long period of neglect'. Paying no heed to the *Telegraph*, Miss Littlewood revived the play five years later at the same theatre, this time employing a set, designed by John Bury, with a 'raked floor of diagonally aligned chequers', which encouraged 'a mannered elaboration'.[24] *The Times* (25 April 1959) tells us that Ann Beach gave a 'clever interpretation' of Franceschina: 'Babyish in her endearments, grovelling in tantrums when discarded, she is little more than spitefully feline.' James Booth gave Freevill 'a knowing rakishness', but Richard Harris was criticised for not giving his Malheureux 'greater motivation'.

The Dutch Courtesan made the English stage again on 14 July 1964, with a National Theatre production by William Gaskill and Piers Haggard. It opened at the Chichester Festival Theatre and later transferred to the Old Vic. Once more the theatre critics were not over-impressed. Philip Hope-Wallace saw it as 'a rather tedious evening' (*The Guardian*, 15 July 1964) and Alan Brien (*The Sunday Telegraph*, 18 October 1964) implied that the play should be left in the study – 'a treat for scholars is too often an ordeal for laymen'. *The Times* critic (15 July) complained that the work did not deserve a revival.[25]

The year 1973 saw the turn of *The Malcontent*, with Jonathan Miller's production at the Nottingham Playhouse[26] (later transferring to London's Bankside Globe). As is to be expected with Miller's work, the production had a firm intellectual and satiric basis. Patrick Robertson's curved set was modelled on Palladio's Teatro Olympico at Vicenza, with rear projections of Vignola's Palazzo Farneze at Caprarola. Between the Palladian arches were the figures of the four humours and the arches themselves were projected through mirrors at the rear. Yet all was shadowy, indistinct and drab. We were in a cobwebbed court fallen to decay. The impression was given of stasis and darkness; even the costumes were made from the same canvas as the set. Faces were whitened and the only touch of colour, the red sashes of the band, came in marked contrast so as to heighten the atmosphere of nausea. Thus a surreal–mannerist quality was achieved through which we gained the chilling knowledge that Malevole's satire was merely another, perhaps the last, manifestation of a futile, decayed and degenerate society. Sexual and political images were nicely mixed and visually juxtaposed to illustrate the decadence into which both had fallen. Critics such as Nicholas de Jongh (*The Guardian*, 14 June 1973), who called it 'a rape . . . of John Marston's tragi-comedy', disapproved, believing with John Peter (*The Sunday Times*, 22 April 1973) that it sacrificed the tragic content of the work to the satiric.[27] Many of the reviewers obviously went to the production with preconceived ideas derived from their own reading of the play and were plainly discontented or, worse, perplexed by an intelligent interpretation which released the play from the 'mouldy fopperies' of the scholastic university-bound imagination. Certainly there were elements in the production which were inconsistent and suspect. As seems to be the case with all Marston productions, the cast was not outstanding, although it was held together by a firm and perceptive performance from Derek Godfrey as Malevole and the creation of a supercilious Mendoza by Michael Johnson. There was, however, far too much movement, which presumably was designed to compensate for lack of experience in some of the repertory players. But on the whole Miller's satiric aim was accomplished, the coldness and decadence were felt by the audience, and Marston's play was invigorated in a manner which possibly was not all that distant from the grotesque mannerism that the original productions may have given it.

Derek Godfrey figured also in the latest Marston production – an adaptation for radio, by Peter Barnes, of the *Antonio* plays.[28] Barnes scored a major success with Jonson's *The Devil is An Ass*, produced at Nottingham during the same season as Miller's *The Malcontent*, and at the Edinburgh Festival, by the Birmingham Repertory Company, in 1976.[29] His work on *Antonio and Mellida* and *Antonio's Revenge* was similarly successful. He adapted the two plays into one two-hour thirty-five-minute production, *Antonio*. So as to gain a consistency throughout, he attempted to reconcile the comedy–tragedy contrast between the two parts by emphasising some of the serious overtones in *Antonio and Mellida* and the comic ones in *Antonio's Revenge*, with the result that the production constantly emphasised the dual perspective which, as we have seen, is at the heart of all Marston's plays. Yet the fact that the production by Martin Esslin was designed for the radio meant that the full surrealist and ritualistic effects of the works could not always be achieved. Thus two crucial scenes, the escape episode (*A & M*, III. ii) and the murder of Julio (*AR*, III. i) were heavily edited. The latter in particular caused a few problems. The ritual aspect was largely ignored in favour of the creation of a banal ghost, which prevented us from believing in Antonio's madness. These, however, were the only important occasions when Esslin and Barnes failed to bridge the tragic–comic gulf. Balurdo, played by Godfrey, became a central figure in their interpretation, his role often reflecting that of Antonio (Edward Petherbridge). At first Balurdo's comedy appeared superficial, but as the play progressed the comic poignancy developed and we began to realise his true relevance. In contrast, Strotzo and Piero delighted in their Machiavellian scheming, with John Philips's Piero often showing the relish of a Marlovian Lightborn. Throughout, the tone was complemented by stately music composed by Carl Davis, who, for Miller's *The Malcontent*, similarly enhanced the interpretation with his arrangements for brass band of works by Gabrieli and Marenzio. The whole, therefore, built towards a final scene in which, for Piero's murder – an execution which in terms of the production seemed to be justified – the comic mask was for the first time totally discarded.

Certainly over the past twenty years Marston has been recognised by the English theatre as a dramatist of a certain significance. It seems that, as he is gradually finding his place back in the repertory, directors and adapters are beginning to realise the potential theatricality in his works; a theatricality depending on a style which thrusts forth a dislocated world not altogether unlike our own.

Abbreviations used for publications cited

A & M	*Antonio and Mellida*
AR	*Antonio's Revenge*
Caputi	Anthony Caputi, *John Marston Satirist* (Ithaca, New York, 1961)
Castiglione	Baldassare Castiglione, *The Book of the Courtier*, trans. Sir Thomas Hoby (1561)
Davenport	*The Poems of John Marston*, ed. Arnold Davenport (Liverpool, 1961)
E in C	*Essays in Criticism*
ELH	*Journal of English Literary History*
Finkelpearl	Philip J. Finkelpearl, *John Marston of the Middle Temple, An Elizabethan Dramatist in His Social Setting* (Cambridge, Mass., 1969)
MLQ	*Modern Language Quarterly*
Montaigne	*The Essayes of Michael Lord of Montaigne done into English by John Florio*, ed. Thomas Seccombe, 3 vols (London, 1908)
N & Q	*Notes & Queries*
PMLA	*Publications of the Modern Language Association of America*
SEL	*Studies in English Literature*
SP	*Studies in Philology*
TLS	*Times Literary Supplement*
Wood	*The Plays of John Marston*, ed. H. Harvey Wood, 3 vols (Edinburgh, 1934–9)

Notes

CHAPTER 1

1. See R. Levin, 'The New *New Inn* and the Proliferation of Good Bad Drama', *E in C*, XXII (1972) pp. 41–7; R. A. Foakes, 'Mr. Levin and "Good Bad Drama"', *E in C*, XXII (1972) pp. 327–9; R. Levin, 'The Proof of Parody', *E in C*, XXIV (1974) pp. 312–17; T. F. Wharton, '*The Malcontent* and Dreams, Visions, Fantasies', *E in C*, XXIV (1974) pp. 261–73; T. F. Wharton, 'Old Marston or New Marston: The *Antonio* Plays', *E in C*, XXV (1975) pp.357–69.
2. See R. A. Foakes: *Shakespeare, The Dark Comedies to the Last Plays: From Satire to Celebration* (London, 1971); 'John Marston's Fantastical Plays: *Antonio and Mellida* and *Antonio's Revenge*', *Philological Quarterly*, XLI (1962) pp. 229–39; 'Tragedy at the Children's Theatre after 1600: A Challenge to the Adult Stage', in *Elizabethan Theatre*, vol. II, ed. D. Galloway (Toronto, 1970) pp. 37–59.
3. Levin, in *E in C*, XXIV, pp. 314–15.
4. See *Meyerhold on Theatre*, trans. and ed. E. Braun (London, 1969) pp. 23–34.
5. The opinion of Ronald Bryden in 'Swinging Away from Stanislavsky's "Seagull"', *Observer Review*, 31 May 1970, p. 28.
6. It is not just a matter of Chekhov or of directors. Ionesco tells us that when he first saw *The Bald Prima Donna* acted he 'was almost surprised to hear the laughter of the audience, who took it all quite happily', since they failed to recognise what he considered to be the play's malaise. *Notes and Counter Notes*, trans. D. Watson (London, 1964) p. 186.
7. This point was forcibly made by Adolph Appia in *Music and the Art of Theatre*, trans. Robert W. Corrigan and Mary Dirks (Miami, 1962). As a result he was led to question drama's integrity as an 'art form'.
8. Constantin Stanislavsky, *An Actor Prepares*, trans. E. Reynolds Hapgood (London, 1937) p. 21: 'You should first of all assimilate the model. This is complicated. You study it from the point of view of the epoch, the time, the country, condition of life, background, literature, psychology, the soul, way of living, social position, and external appearance; moreover, you study character, such as custom, manner, movements, voice, speech, intonations. All this work on your material will help you permeate it with your own feelings. Without all this you will have no art.'
9. Hunter's interpretations are found mainly in his introductions to various editions of Marston's plays cited below, and in 'English Folly and Italian Vice: The Moral Landscape of John Marston', *Stratford-*

upon-Avon Studies, I (London, 1960) pp. 85–111. Foakes's views are found in the works of his cited in notes 1 and 2 above.

10. Anthony Caputi, *John Marston, Satirist* (Ithaca, NY, 1961).
11. See Ch. 8 below.
12. As there is no standard edition of Marston's drama, I shall employ for reference the best individual editions of the plays. These will be cited in the notes as they occur. Reavley Gair's edition of *Antonio's Revenge*, The Revels Plays (Manchester, 1978), had not been published when the present work went to press.

CHAPTER 2

1. *An Actor Prepares*, p. 156. Plato states the problem in *The Republic*, trans. F. M. Cornford (Oxford, 1941) p. 330: 'Few, I believe, are capable of reflecting that to enter into another's feelings must have an effect on our own: the emotions of pity our sympathy has strengthened will not be easy to restrain when we are suffering ourselves.' The concern is often discussed in English Renaissance drama. See, for example, Massinger's *The Roman Actor* (1626), IV. ii. 30–52, as well as many of Shakespeare's plays: for instance, *A Midsummer Night's Dream*, III. i. 25–42, and *Hamlet*, II. ii. 542–63. Shakespeare references throughout are to the Alexander text, Collins edition (London, 1951).
2. References to *Antonio and Mellida* and *Antonio's Revenge* are to G. K. Hunter's editions, Regent Renaissance Drama Series (London, 1965 and 1966). Ellen Berland, in 'The Function of Irony in Marston's *Antonio and Mellida*', *SP*, LXVI (1969) p. 741, writes of the relationship of actor to part and actor to audience: 'The audience [can be] aware not only of the actor impersonating a dramatic character but also of that character impersonating another one. The character, himself, an actor in the real world, becomes an actor in the imaginary world of the play.'
3. Introduction, *Antonio's Revenge*, p. xii.
4. Hunter, in *Stratford-upon-Avon Studies*, I, p. 100.
5. See Hunter, Introduction to *Antonio and Mellida*, p. xiv. Ellen Berland, in *SP*, LXVI, p. 751, also notes, 'If Feliche were as content and as honest as he pretends to be, he would have no reason to remain at court. Once he had proved to himself that he was not envious of court life, he would leave. As he is, however, he remains there, like a detached scientist observing the data, i.e. "the nocturnall court delights," in order to test his own attitude. His self-revelations to Castilio indicate further the contradiction between his assumed manner and his true character.'
6. Compare, for example, the way in which eighteenth-century authors juxtapose the Stoicism of such characters with disastrous occurrence, so destroying their patronising attitude. See Fielding, *Joseph Andrews*, Bk IV, ch. 8; Goldsmith, *The Vicar of Wakefield*, ch. 28; Johnson, *Rasselas*, ch. 18.
7. T. S. Eliot, *Elizabethan Dramatists* (London, 1963) p. 157.
8. See, for example, *Antonio's Revenge*, I. i. 9–12; II. ii. 214–24.
9. The only clue given for his deeds comes in *Antonio's Revenge*, I. i. 23–9,

where he talks of his jealousy caused by Andrugio's marriage with Maria.
10. H. Harvey Wood, Introduction to *The Plays of John Marston*, 3 vols (London and Edinburgh, 1934–9) vol. I, p. xxii.
11. Philip J. Ayres, 'Marston's *Antonio's Revenge*: The Morality of the Revenging Hero', *SEL*, XII (1972) p. 367.
12. John Peter, *Complaint and Satire in Early English Literature* (Oxford, 1956) p. 224.
13. *A & M*, II. i. 200, III. ii. 184, IV. i. 28, IV. i. 165.
14. *A & M*, III. i. 39.
15. See Hunter, Introduction to *Antonio and Mellida*, p. xix.
16. Sir Thomas Elyot, *The Castel of Helth* (1541), Scholar's Facsimiles and Reprints (New York, 1936) p. 2, tells us, 'The Bodye, where heate and moysture haue souerayntie, is called *Sanguine*, wherein the Ayre hath preeminence.'
17. Hunter, Introduction to *Antonio's Revenge*, p. xvii.
18. From a fifth-century homily quoted in O. B. Hardison Jr, *Christian Rite and Christian Drama in the Middle Ages. Essays in the Origin and Early History of Modern Drama* (Baltimore, 1965) p. 37.
19. A. P. Rossiter, *English Drama from Early Times to the Elizabethans* (London, 1950) p. 17, is one of many writers to tell us that, 'in the drunken orgy of the bacchanal or the sexual orgy of the primitive fertility-cult, the gods not only show their power but *are*, as their true selves, in the frenzies of intoxication or of animal lust'. J. G. Frazer, in *The Golden Bough* (London, 1951) p. 124, gives examples but notes, 'examples of such temporary inspiration are so common in every part of the world and are now so familiar through books on ethnology that it is needless to multiply illustrations of the general principle'.
20. Ayres, in *SEL*, XII, p. 362. Wood, in his Introduction to *The Plays of John Marston*, vol. I, p. xxxvi, cites the episode as an example of Marston failing to have 'a refinement of art (and justice)'. R. A. Foakes, in an alternative approach to the play, discusses this scene in the context of the satire on the productions of the adult companies: 'The deliberate disregard for moral consistency goes together with another reminder that the actors are choirboys playing in the "holy verge" of Saint Paul's. This last scene can only be interpreted as consciously outrageous, flouting with calculated enormity a conventional ending which would have punished Antonio.' See his *Shakespeare, The Dark comedies to the Last Plays*, pp. 69–70.
21. Hunter, Introduction to *Antonio's Revenge*, p. ix.
22. Ibid.
23. Philip Finkelpearl, in *John Marston of the Middle Temple, An Elizabethan Dramatist in His Social Setting* (Cambridge, Mass., 1969) p. 159, notes, 'there is no one to punish them [the revengers], no one to establish a new order in Venice after the convulsion, for Marston is describing a general condition. This is what "men were, and are, [and] . . . must be"'.
24. Neither play, of course, had been written at the time *Antonio's Revenge* appeared.

25. Hunter, in *Stratford-upon-Avon Studies*, I, p. 86.
26. Hunter, Introduction to *Antonio's Revenge*, p. xvii.

CHAPTER 3

1. References to *The Malcontent* are to G. K. Hunter's edition, The Revels Plays (London, 1975).
2. See, for example, Peter, *Complaint and Satire*, p. 238: 'its chief challenge to the dramatist is in the matter of integration. Yet in two very important respects Marston has failed to meet the challenge satisfactorily: the structure of the play is defective, and so is the conception of its chief character, Malevole.' Eliot, *Elizabethan Dramatists*, p. 160: 'The whole part is inadequately thought out; Malevole is either too important or not important enough.' Wharton, in *E in C*, XXIV, p. 273: 'In one case, that of the lecher Ferneze, Marston cannot even trouble himself to make repentance convincing.'
3. Hunter, Introduction to *The Malcontent*, p. lxiv. Hunter notes in particular the influence of Guarini's *Il Pastor Fido* on Marston's play. Referring to the title page of Ben Jonson's 1616 folio, which 'provides an excellent diagram' of the relationship between Satyr, Pastor and Tragicomoedia, Hunter proposes that, although *The Malcontent* is 'totally unpastoral', it 'makes good sense if we assume that [Marston] sought to transfer the principal weight of tragicomedy from the pastoral foot to the satyric' (pp. lxiii–lxiv).
4. See, for example, Hunter's Introduction to *Antonio and Mellida*, pp. xviii–xix, and Martin L. Wine, Introduction to *The Malcontent*, Regents Renaissance Drama Series (London, 1965) pp. xxiv–xxv.
5. See, for example, Wharton, in *E in C*, XXIV, p. 268: 'The problem is to decide how far all this is a deliberate tactical manoeuvre by Altofronto, in his disguise as Malevole, and how far Altofronto himself may be identified with his persona.'
6. Ibid., pp. 261–2. Wharton's essay is particularly informative in its discussion of Mendoza's role-play.
7. *The Malcontent*, ed. Hunter, p. 20.
8. Jean Genet, *The Balcony*, trans. B. Frechtman (London, 1966) p. 10.
9. Finkelpearl, *John Marston of the Middle Temple*, p. 185.
10. Caputi, in *John Marston, Satirist*, p. 192, notes, 'Except in Act IV . . . practically every incident of serious matter is accompanied by or followed immediately by a brief explosion of light immoral grotesquery.' Finkelpearl, in *John Marston of the Middle Temple*, p.190, draws an interesting parallel between Malevole and Maquerelle: 'She plays Lady Fortune in sexual matters . . . just as Malevole manipulates political fortunes.'
11. Francis A. Schaeffer, *Escape from Reason* (London, 1968) p. 67.
12. 'The Scourge of Villanie, Satyre II', 1–6, in *The Poems of John Marston*, ed. Arnold Davenport (Liverpool, 1961) p. 106. All references to Marston's poems are to this edition.
13. Jean-Paul Sartre, 'In Camera', in *Two Plays by Jean-Paul Sartre*, trans. S. Gilbert (London, 1946) p. 145.

14. *Montaigne: Essays*, trans. J. Florio (1603), selected and introduced by Andre Gide, Introduction trans. Dorothy Bussy (New York, 1965) p. 10.
15. Caputi, *John Marston, Satirist*, p. 241.
16. Peter Ure, 'John Marston's *Sophonisba*: A Reconsideration', *Durham University Journal*, New. Ser., x (1948–9) pp. 81–90, repr. in *Elizabethan and Jacobean Drama: Critical Essays by Peter Ure* ed. J. C. Maxwell (Liverpool, 1974) pp. 75–92.
17. Page references to *Sophonisba* are to H. Harvey Wood's edition (*The Plays of John Marston*, vol. II, pp. 1–64).
18. Machiavelli saw nothing wrong in virtue and *virtù* co-existing as long as virtue remained subservient. In *The Prince*, trans. W. K. Marriot (London, 1908) p. 142, he warns, 'a wise lord cannot, nor ought he to, keep faith when such observance may be turned against him, and when reasons that caused him to pledge it exist no longer'.

CHAPTER 4

1. Ure, in *Durham University Journal*, New. Ser., x, p. 77.
2. References to *The Dutch Courtesan* are to Martin L. Wine's edition, Regents Renaissance Drama Series (London, 1965).
3. Baldassare Castiglione, *The Book of the Courtier*, trans. Sir Thomas Hoby (1561), introd. J. H. Whitfield (London, 1974).
4. Montaigne, *The Essayes*, trans. John Florio (1603), ed. Thomas Seccombe, 3 vols (London, 1908). The essays are referred to by book and chapter.
5. A fuller summary of the story is to be found in John J. O'Connor, 'The Chief Source of Marston's *Dutch Courtezan*', *SP*, LIV (1957) pp. 509–15.
6. Castiglione, *The Book of the Courtier*, p. 309.
7. My view is at variance with that of T. S. Eliot, who in *Elizabethan Dramatists*, p. 158, holds that Franceschina's 'isolation is enhanced by her broken English'. As mentioned in Ch. 6, I believe that in isolating evil by linguistic means Marston was employing a technique common on the medieval stage.
8. *The Poems of John Marston*, ed. Davenport, p. 56.
9. Caputi, *John Marston, Satirist*, p. 234.
10. William Empson, *Some Versions of Pastoral* (London, 1935) p. 34.
11. Finkelpearl, *John Marston of the Middle Temple*, pp. 215–16. See also Peter H. Davison, Introduction to *The Dutch Courtesan*, The Fountainwell Drama Texts (Berkeley and Los Angeles, 1968) p. 7: 'all Cocledemoy's activities are comic . . . [He] is the principal means whereby the comic aspects of venery and defecation are expressed, and he instigates the grotesquely comic attempt to make a bargain with Mistress Mulligrub for her "other things" as her husband is on the way to the scaffold.

    'More important, however, and overlooked by those who complain of a lack of relationship between the main and sub-plots, Cocledemoy is a *comic* version of Freevill – of the man who has come to terms with sexual desires.'
12. Gustav Cross, in 'Marston, Montaigne and Morality: *The Dutch Courtezan* Reconsidered', *ELH*, XXVII (1960) pp. 30–43, takes an opposite view,

since he holds that 'we feel only that justice has been done [when] at the end of the play, she [Franceschina] is led off to "the extreamest whip and jaile" '. Cross, however, never attacks the Montaigne philosophy and consequently describes the libertine's actions without question: 'Freevill, who accepts the "naturalness" of sexuality, regards Franceschina simply as a "saleable commodity," and can therefore permit himself physical indulgence without becoming a slave to passion.'

13. See, for example, 'Satyre VIII', in *The Poems of John Marston*, ed. Davenport, pp. 150–7.
14. O'Connor, in *SP*, LIV, pp. 514–15.
15. Caputi, in *John Marston, Satirist*, p. 271, tells us, 'no solution to the problem of authorship can be advanced with confidence until a thorough study has been made of the play's manifold textual problems, and even then the play could well remain a tantalizing conundrum'.
16. Page references to *The Insatiate Countess* are to H. Harvey Wood's edition (*The Plays of John Marston*, vol. III, pp. 1–82).
17. See, for example, Shakespeare's adaptation of the popular song 'Mistress Mine' in *Twelfth Night*, II. iii. 38–51.
18. See my hypothesis that Marston possibly wrote the first draft of the play in 1602/3 – *N & Q*, New. Ser. XXIV, (1977) pp. 116–17.

CHAPTER 5

1. M. C. Andrews, 'Jack Drum's Entertainment *as Burlesque*', *Renaissance Quarterly*, XXIV (1971) p. 226.
2. Ibid., p. 228.
3. Critical Introduction to *The Comedy of Errors*, ed. R. A. Foakes, New Arden (London, 1962) pp. xxxix–li. Foakes, however, is still wary of the danger of seeing too much depth in the play.
4. For a brief discussion of Levin's views see above, Ch. 1.
5. Caputi, *John Marston, Satirist*, pp. 124, 127.
6. Williams's famous production of *The Comedy of Errors*, which drew parallels with the *commedia dell 'arte*, was first seen in Stratford during the 1962 season. It subsequently went on European and American tours and was most recently revived by the Royal Shakespeare Company in 1972.
7. These lines are quoted by all the major critics of the work who are in agreement that they are a statement of the play's satiric intention. Page references to *Jack Drum's Entertainment* are to H. Harvey Wood's edition (*The Plays of John Marston*, vol. III, pp. 179–240).
8. Finkelpearl, in *John Marston of the Middle Temple*, pp. 125–39, goes to great lengths in an attempt to connect the Marston caricatures with contemporary characters in the Highgate district of London. It is an interesting hypothesis, but again we must apply reservations, since there is not enough real evidence to state anything with certainty.
9. The comic balcony scene appears in numerous Renaissance plays. Marston was particularly fond of it, as we discover not only on the four

occasions it is employed in *Jack Drum*, but also on its use in *Antonio and Mellida*, *The Insatiate Countess* and *The Fawn*.

10. L. C. Knights, *Drama and Society in the Age of Jonson* (London, 1937).
11. Page references to *What You Will* are to H. Harvey Wood's edition (*The Plays of John Marston*, vol. II, pp. 230–95).
12. It is an interesting fact that the most recent revival in Britain of a Marston play in the professional theatre was brought about by the collaboration of two of these wits. John Wells adapted *The Malcontent* for Jonathan Miller's 1973 production. See below, Ch. 8.
13. Finkelpearl, *John Marston of the Middle Temple*, p. 165.
14. Ibid., p. 164.
15. Ibid.: 'I am not suggesting that Marston was representing himself on stage, merely that Lampatho embodies some of his traits and almost none of Jonson's.'
16. See, for example, A. Harbage, *Shakespeare and the Rival Traditions* (Bloomington, Ind., and London, 1970) p. 162. Harbage cites Morse S. Allen, *The Satire of John Marston* (Columbus, Ohio, 1920) p. 138, which sees Quadratus as 'a curious mixture of stoicism and epicureanism'.
17. The resemblance has also been noted by Caputi, in *John Marston, Satirist*, p. 170. Finkelpearl, in *John Marston of the Middle Temple*, p. 177, draws similar parallels with Sir Toby Belch.
18. Leslie Hotson, *The First Night of Twelfth Night* (London, 1954) p. 158, too easily dismisses the festive element implied by Marston's title. Finkelpearl, in *John Marston of the Middle Temple*, pp. 176–7, sees 'superficial resemblances' between the Marston and Shakespeare plays.
19. Joel Kaplan, 'John Marston's *Fawn*: A Saturnalian Satire', *SEL*, IX (1969) p. 343.
20. References to *The Fawn* are to Gerald A. Smith's edition, Regents Renaissance Drama Series (London, 1965).
21. E. H. Kantorowicz, *The King's Two Bodies, A Study in Mediaeval Political Theology* (Princeton, 1957).
22. See Kaplan, in *SEL*, IX, pp. 339–40, for an interesting interpretation of Hercules's intentions at the beginning of the play.
23. Ibid., pp. 337–8.
24. There is one significant technical mistake. At the end of the play, Marston seems to forget about Philocalia.

CHAPTER 6

1. For example Hunter, Introduction to *The Malcontent*, p. lxxx, comments, 'The whole structure of the play is concerned with speeches, passions, and persuasions which are rendered unreal by a context which highlights their manner rather than their matter'. See also Donna B. Hamilton, 'Language as Theme in *The Dutch Courtesan*', *Renaissance Drama*, V (1972) pp. 75–87.
2. Theodore Spencer, 'John Marston', *The Criterion*, XIII, no. 53 (1934) pp. 583–4.
3. Charles Lamb, *Specimens of English Dramatic Poets* (London, 1897) p. 66.

4. Terence Hawkes, *Shakespeare's Talking Animals* (London, 1973) p. 27.
5. Una Ellis Fermor, *The Jacobean Drama*, 5th edition (London, 1965) p. 78. Miss Fermor's approach has also been followed by Ejner J. Jensen in 'Theme and Imagery in *The Malcontent*', *SEL*, x (1970) pp. 367–84.
6. *Mundus et Infans*, in *Specimens of the Pre-Shakespearean Drama*, ed. J. M. Manly, 2 vols (New York, 1967) vol. I. Compare, for example, lines 76–122 with lines 237–87.
7. W. Wager, *Enough Is as Good as a Feast*, 306–17, in *English Morality Plays and Moral Interludes*, ed. T. Schell and J. D. Shuchter (New York, 1969).
8. Peter Brook, *The Empty Space*, Pelican edition (London, 1972) p. 59.
9. Ibid., p. 55.
10. A. C. Swinburne, *The Age of Shakespeare* (London, 1908) pp. 145–6.
11. Eliot, *Elizabethan Dramatists*, p. 156.
12. See above, Ch. 2.
13. Touchstone makes this point quite clear in *As You Like It*, II. iv. 43–52: 'I remember, when I was in love, I broke my sword upon a stone, and bid him take that for coming a-night to Jane Smile; and I remember the kissing of her batler, and the cow's dugs that her pretty chopt hands had milk'd; and I remember the wooing of a peascod instead of her; from whom I took two cods, and, giving her them again, said with weeping tears "Wear these for my sake". We that are true lovers run into strange capers; but as all is mortal in nature, so is all nature in love mortal in folly.'
14. Ironically, the words of T. S. Eliot in 'To My Wife', *The Complete Poems and Plays* (London, 1969) p. 522.
15. Wharton, in 'Old Marston or New Marston: The *Antonio* Plays', *E in C*, xxv, pp. 357–69, takes an opposite view to the one I am proposing. From finding some linguistic examples of 'stylistic opportunism' he moves to a conclusion which 'demonstrates his [Marston's] incapacity to handle plot and agent in any integrated design'. I hope my comments on the verbal language and imagery in the *Antonio* plays may rather be seen in the context of the author's dramatic method throughout the works, as discussed in Chs. 2 and 7.
16. Samuel Schoenbaum, 'The Precarious Balance of John Marston', *PMLA*, LXVII (1952) pp. 1069–78, repr. in *Elizabethan Drama*, ed. Ralph J. Kaufman (London, Oxford, New York, 1961) pp. 123–33. Others with similar views to Schoenbaum include Morse S. Allen, who in *The Satire of John Marston*, p. 97, writes, 'When lust is so carefully and lingeringly dwelt upon, it is impossible to avoid the suspicion that its consideration was pleasing to the author. There is no reason for doubting that such was the case.' See also Rupert Brook, *John Webster and the Elizabethan Drama* (London, 1916) p. 69: 'He loved dirt for truth's sake; also for its own.'
17. Montaigne, *Essayes*, Bk III, ch. 5.

CHAPTER 7

1. Hunter, Introduction to *Antonio and Mellida*, p. xvii.
2. *The Complete Works of John Lyly*, ed. R. Warwick Bond, 3 vols (Oxford, 1902) vol. II, p. 372.

3. Anon., *The Taming of A Shrew*, in *Narrative and Dramatic Sources of Shakespeare*, ed. G. Bullough, vol. I (London and New York, 1957) p. 108.
4. M. C. Bradbrook, *English Dramatic Form in the Old Drama and the New*, 2nd edition (London, 1970) p. 71.
5. Ibid., pp. 30–1.
6. A. Artaud, *The Theatre and Its Double*, trans. Victor Corti (London, 1970) pp. 70–1.
7. Ibid., p. 71.
8. André Breton's first Surrealist Manifesto (1924); see Werner Haftmann, *Painting in the Twentieth Century*, trans. Ralph Manheim, 2nd edition, 2 vols (London, 1965) vol. I, p. 188.
9. 'Certain Satyres', I. 123–4.
10. Christian Kiefer, 'Music and Marston's *The Malcontent*', *SP*, LI (1954) p. 165. In the same article, p. 166, Kiefer proposes, 'That discordant music is the appropriate music for the corrupt society of the Genoese court is a concept which continues throughout the play, serving to broaden and organize the satiric attack.'
11. Sir Thomas Elyot, *The Boke Named The Gouernour* (1531), ed. H. H. S. Croft (London, 1883) Bk I, ch. 21, pp. 235–6, 238.
12. Castiglione, *The Book of the Courtier*, p. 101.
13. Ibid., p. 98.
14. *The Poems of John Marston*, ed. Davenport, p. 356.
15. 'The Scourge of Villanie, Satire XI', 15–20, 23–4. See also 'Certain Satyres', I. 125–36.
16. See above, Ch. 2; also Hunter, Introduction to *Antonio and Mellida*, p. xiv.
17. Bernard Harris, in his Introduction to *The Malcontent*, The New Mermaids edition (London, 1967) p. xvi, notes, 'The music to *The Malcontent* has not survived, and with it has been lost a necessary element in the process of preparing, adjusting, or "keying" audience-response.'
18. Dieter Mehl, *The Elizabethan Dumb Show, the History of a Dramatic Convention* (London, 1965) pp. 124–5.
19. John Reibetanz, 'Hieronimo in Decimosexto', *Renaissance Drama*, V (1972) p. 94, gives an alternative interpretation of this scene, seeing it as a 'clever burlesque around the famous "Painter Scene"' of Kyd's *The Spanish Tragedy*, 'with its search to express the inexpressible through visual emblems'. See also 'Marston's Parodies of the Painter Scene', Appendix E to *The Spanish Tragedy*, ed. Philip Edwards, The Revels Plays (London, 1969).
20. Preface, *Antonio and Mellida*.

CHAPTER 8

1. Mehl, *The Elizabethan Dumb Show*, p. 123.
2. Page references to *Histriomastix* are to the H. Harvey Wood edition (*The Plays of John Marston*, vol. III, pp. 243–302). Although for a long time it was thought that Marston only revised this play, it has been argued by

Alvin Kernan, in 'John Marston's Play *Histriomastix*', *MLQ*, XIX (1958) pp. 134–140, and by Finkelpearl, in *John Marston of the Middle Temple*, pp. 119–24, that the whole play may be attributed to him. Finkelpearl interestingly contends that the work was written by Marston neither for the public nor for the private theatres, but rather for the Inns of Court Christmas revels, 1598–9. As such he sees it as a 'quasi-pageant for the edification and glorification of his [Marston's] Society and of his Queen'. Caputi, in *John Marston, Satirist*, pp. 80–116, following the theory that Marston's hand is evident only from Act III onwards, proposes that, as an old play which Marston was able to 'refurbish', *Histriomastix* 'offered him unusual opportunities to indulge the satiric and didactic propensities' seen in the earlier poems. As such *Histriomastix* is regarded as a transitional work between Marston's poetic and dramatic periods of writing. J. Scott-Colley, in *John Marston's Theatrical Drama* (Salzburg, 1974), pp. 32–46, considers the work to be as much about 'acting' and 'role-playing' as anything else. Little more can or perhaps should be said until a full textual study and edition of the play appears.

3. The problem is obviously still with us. Jonathan Miller tells me that the idea behind his 1973 production of *The Malcontent* would have been different if he had employed a boys' company. Interestingly enough, he has attempted to persuade St Paul's school to present the play – so far without success. His concept of a juvenile production would be to present the play in terms of Jarry's *Ubu Roi*.
4. *Hamlet*, II. ii. 334.
5. Hunter, in his Introduction to *The Malcontent*, p. xlix, notes, 'That the augmentations of the play text were written in part or in whole by Marston is, to me, clear beyond doubt. I believe that it would be possible to make this point in terms of style alone.'
6. Ibid., p. lii.
7. Ibid., p. li.
8. The omission is at I. iii. 0. 1. I follow Hunter's supposition that 'QA and QB . . . represent the Blackfriars version, and QC the Globe version' (Hunter, Introduction to *The Malcontent*, p. lxxxi).
9. Kiefer, in *SP*, LI, p. 170.
10. Above, Chs 3 and 7.
11. Miller's Nottingham production opened in a similar fashion, with a brass band playing an overture which was then rudely imitated by Malevole.
12. See above, Ch. 3.
13. Caputi, *John Marston, Satirist*, p. 275.
14. E. K. Chambers, *The Elizabethan Stage*, 4 vols (Oxford, 1923) vol. III, p. 431 and vol. IV, pp. 180 and 182.
15. G. E. Bentley, *The Jacobean and Caroline Stage*, 7 vols (Oxford, 1941) vol. I, p. 123.
16. See Francis Kirkman, *The Wits or Sport upon Sport* (1673), ed. John James Elson (Ithaca, NY, 1932) pp. 346–67.
17. See, Leo Hughes and Arthur H. Scouten, 'Some Theatrical Adaptations of a Picaresque Tale', *Studies in English* (Austin, Texas, 1945–6) p. 102.
18. As the printed edition of the work (London, 1680) bears no name its

authorship is uncertain. Some, including the British Museum, ascribe the play to Thomas Betterton, a man who was not averse to stage adaptations, since, for example, he did act Tate's version of *King Lear*. Others, however, favour Mrs Aphra Behn as the author. In a letter to me Martin Wine has kindly given evidence both for and against the respective claims: 'Although Gerard Langbaine as early as 1691 observed "this play [*The Revenge*] is ascribed to Mrs. Behn, but is indeed a play of Marston's revived, and called *The Dutch Courtesan*" (*Account of the English Dramatic Poets*, Oxford 1691, p. 547), most historians of the English theatre – as Reed, Baker, Dibdin, Doran, Lowe, to name a few – have claimed Betterton for its author. They may have taken their lead from an early historical account, the anonymous *A Comparison between the Two Stages* (London, 1702), which attributed to Betterton the adaptation of *The Vintner Trick'd; Or, A Match in Newgate* – probably the same play or a slightly modified version of it (see Staring B. Well's edition of *A Comparison*, Princeton 1942, pp. 11, 123–4). In recent times, however, William Van Lennep has discovered that Narcissus Luttrell has written in his copy of the play the date purchased as July 6, 1680, and the name of its author as "Mrs. Aphra Behn", warranting the conclusion that the play was acted before that date and that Langbaine's information was correct. See Van Lennep's letter "Two Restoration Comedies", in *TLS*, January 28, 1939, pp. 57–8.'

19. O'Connor, in *SP*, LIV, p. 513.
20. Dashit, we are told, cheated him out of a £200-a-year estate.
21. Christopher Bullock, *A Woman's Revenge; or A Match in Newgate* (London, 1715) p. 56.
22. See Hughes and Scouten, in *Studies in English*, pp. 98–114.
23. *The Times*, 24 Feb. 1954. Harry Corbett played Freevill and Howard Goorney, Malheureux.
24. *The Times*, 25 Apr. 1959.
25. The cast included Billie Whitelaw as Franceschina; Frank Finlay, Cocledemoy; John Stride, Freevill; and George Innes, Malheureux.
26. First performance 11 Apr. 1973.
27. In a later *Sunday Times* review (17 June 1973), J. W. Lambert argued against de Jongh, Peter and others, 'Mr. Miller has been under fire for turning what the play's first printer billed as a tragi-comedy into a satirical farce. But he is quite right to do so. Marston used the framework of conventional revenge–tragedy to mock not only corruption in high quarters but the theatrical appetite which demanded violent action, and debased humanity in the process.'
28. BBC Radio 3, 20 Feb. 1977.
29. The production had a short season at The National Theatre in 1977.

Index